GETTING STARTED

with

RIGOROUS CURRICULUM DESIGN

**How School Districts Are Successfully
Redesigning Their Curricula
for the Common Core**

GETTING STARTED

with

RIGOROUS CURRICULUM DESIGN

How School Districts Are Successfully
Redesigning Their Curricula
for the Common Core

LARRY AINSWORTH

KRISTIN R. ANDERSON

LEAD+
LEARN
PRESS

ENGLEWOOD, COLORADO

The Leadership and Learning Center
317 Inverness Way South, Suite 150
Englewood, Colorado 80112
Phone 1.866.399.6019 | Fax 303.504.9417
www.LeadandLearn.com

ISBN 978-1-935588-40-5
Printed in the United States of America

17 16 15 14 13   01 02 03 04 05 06 07

Contents

About the Authors

 **Larry Ainsworth** is the Executive Director of Professional Development at The Leadership and Learning Center in Englewood, Colorado. He travels nationally and internationally to assist school systems in implementing best practices related to standards, assessment, curriculum, and instruction across all grades and content areas. He is the author or

(2010), *"Unwrapping" the Standards* (2003b), *Power Standards* (2003a), *Common Formative Assessments* (2006), *Five Easy Steps to a Balanced Math Program* (2000), and *Student Generated Rubrics* (1998). Larry regularly works on site in school systems to assist leaders and educators in understanding and implementing standards-based practices: prioritizing and "unwrapping" the standards, developing common formative assessments, designing authentic performance tasks, and creating rigorous curricular units of study in all content areas, prekindergarten through grade 12. He has keynoted for schools, districts, and widely respected organizations around the world.

With 24 years of experience as an upper elementary and middle school classroom teacher in demographically diverse schools, Larry brings a varied background and wide range of professional experiences to each of his presentations. He has held numerous leadership roles within school districts, including mentor teacher and K–12 math committee cochair, and has served as a mathematics assessment consultant in several San Diego County school districts. Larry holds a master's degree in educational administration.

 **Kristin R. Anderson** began her career as a high school English teacher for students who were kicked out of Denver Public Schools. Since then, she has worked in multiple K–12 settings in various instructional and administrative roles, and has obtained advanced degrees from Sterling College in Sterling, Kansas, The University of Denver, and The University of Colorado in Colorado Springs. She is a longtime student of the field, a passionate educator, and an inspirational leader. Kristin is the author of *Data Teams Success Stories Volume 1* (2010) and *Real-Time Decisions* (2012), and currently serves as Director of Professional Learning with Corwin Press in Thousand Oaks, California. She resides in Castle Rock, Colorado, with her husband of over 14 years and two children.

Acknowledgments

Thank you to the following people who made this book happen, for taking the initiative to make comprehensive unit planning a priority and for sharing the start of your journey with all of us:

- Sally Alubicki, Ed.D.—Director of Teaching and Assessment, West Hartford Public Schools, West Hartford, Connecticut

- Tracy Chambers—Director of Professional Development, Hemet Unified School District, Riverside County, California

- Kyra Donovan—Director of Elementary and Federal Programs, McMinnville School District, McMinnville, Oregon

- Anne P. Druzolowski, Ph.D.—Assistant Superintendent of Schools, West Haven Public Schools, West Haven, Connecticut

- Teresa Healy—Assistant Superintendent Education Services, Barstow Unified School District, San Bernardino County, California

- David Horton, Ed.D.—Director of Accountability, Hemet Unified School District, Riverside County, California

- Mary O'Neil Grace, Ed.D.—Assistant Superintendent, Education Services, Anaheim City School District, Orange County, California

- Janie Pyle, Ed.D.—Associate Superintendent, Raytown Quality Schools, Raytown, Missouri

- LeeAnn Segalla—Executive Director, Guilford County Schools, Guilford, North Carolina

- Ellen J. Stoltz, Ph.D.— Chief Academic Officer, Office of Instructional Leadership, Bloomfield Public Schools, Bloomfield, Connecticut.

Thank you as well to the many courageous educators that contributed to the development of their district's curricular units of study: team members, the schools' support staff members, and the administrations that made brave decisions to invest in professional development, monitor implementation, and champion the process throughout.

Finally, thank you to The Leadership and Learning Center Professional Development Associates who have worked diligently with schools and districts across the country in planning for and implementing the Common Core State Standards using the Rigorous Curriculum Design model. Without you, none of this would have taken shape or come to life.

Introduction

"Rigorous Curriculum Design should be a required course in every teacher education program in the country. Without it, educators will never see the whole picture that makes up their professional career."

GARY L. SACKET,
AURORA LEARNING COMMUNITY ASSOCIATION, FAIRVIEW, OKLAHOMA

This powerful quote is just one representative sample of the positive feedback we continue to receive from school districts around the nation that have been actively implementing the Rigorous Curriculum Design (RCD) model in order to rewrite their English language arts and math curricula to meet the demands of the Common Core State Standards (CCSS).

Although the RCD model was not created specifically to address the CCSS (the book was first published in July 2010—only one month after the release of the new standards), its practical, step-by-step approach to developing robust curricular units of study aligned to the Common Core has attracted the attention of educators and leaders throughout the country.

Yet the real sense of urgency compelling school systems to dramatically overhaul their curricula is in great part due to the new national assessments aligned to the Common Core now being developed by two major assessment consortia: the Partnership for Assessment of Readiness for College and Careers (PARCC) and the Smarter Balanced Assessment Consortium (SBAC). This sense of urgency will continue to increase as we approach 2014/15—the school year in which students within the 46 states (as well as the District of Columbia, Guam, and the U.S. Virgin Islands) that have adopted the Common Core will first sit for these decidedly more rigorous exams.

Don't Wait to Implement

Since the official launch of the Common Core in 2010—and even before there was much focus on the new national assessments—we at The Leadership and Learning Center began advocating the following message to all of the school systems and educators we serve: "Begin now. Don't wait to implement the Common Core." We have been saying this repeatedly because the increased rigor in these new standards is causing educators to completely rethink how they will teach and assess their students' understanding of them. These sometimes seismic paradigm shifts in thinking will continue to result in dramatic changes to our longstanding curriculum, instruction, and assessment practices.

Like most educators, we have been following the assessment information incrementally published by both assessment consortia. The Model Content Frameworks of PARCC and the Content Specifications produced by SBAC are providing their member states with increasingly specific information as to how students will be assessed, accompanied by grade-level sample prototypes of test questions. Educators and leaders in all Common Core states need to keep abreast of the continuing publications coming forth from these two consortia, paying particular attention to the formatting, academic language, rigor, and types of questions students will encounter. They should begin *now* to incorporate these same elements into school and district assessments in order to help students make the transition *later*.

A third set of documents of major importance to all educators and leaders is "The Publishers' Criteria for the Common Core State Standards," written for K–12 English language arts and for K–8 mathematics. These documents provide clear and exceedingly helpful guidelines that school systems should continue to refer to when selecting appropriate materials and resources to implement the CCSS. They are a perfect accompaniment to the unit design steps in the RCD process.

Because the Common Core standards and the coming new assessments are entirely changing the educational landscape as we have known it, our message to districts and schools continues to be: "Don't wait to implement." Educators and leaders need time and focused professional development to really get to know these standards and how they will be assessed: by reading, questioning, discussing, processing, and applying the Common Core in the context of the PARCC and SBAC guiding documents. Even though the reauthorization of "No Child Left Behind" remains stalled in Congress, and states are being granted waivers for reporting student progress, it is unlikely that we will see a lessening of emphasis on high-stakes standardized testing in the Common Core years. Unless there is a sudden reversal of the current testing trajectory, how our nation's students perform on the new national assessments will remain the primary accountability measure for our educators.

We write this not to alarm or frighten, but rather to raise awareness. Every district group that we have led through the RCD process—a process that reveals just how different the Common Core standards really are when compared to state standards—has said, in so many words, "How will districts that are waiting to implement these standards ever be ready in time?"

Curriculum: The Central Focus

In April 2012, Larry experienced a major "aha" moment while in Connecticut (a governing state of the Smarter Balanced Assessment Consortium). He was there to facilitate the Rigorous Curriculum Design process in West Haven (the district he proudly refers to as "the birthplace of RCD") and in West Hartford (the district that rightfully prides itself on high achievement in its student body representing 65 different languages). Teams of K–12 educators in English language arts and math diligently collaborated with their respective grade-span design teams to create units of study. In addition, teams of secondary science and history/social studies educators were present to prioritize the 6–12 Common Core literacy standards for their respective content areas and then to incorporate into their existing units of study these prioritized literacy standards.

While studying the SBAC materials that preview the kinds of cognitively demanding performance task questions students are likely to be presented with in 2014/15, Larry realized that it is the *curriculum* that educators must rely upon to prepare students for these significantly more challenging exams. And therefore the development of a strong curriculum must become the central focus of our educators' efforts to effectively implement the Common Core. If our curricular units fall short in their quality and rigor, students will not acquire the depth of knowledge, skills, and mental stamina needed to demonstrate proficiency on these exams—whether from SBAC or from PARCC.

School systems will greatly serve their educators and leaders by making available to them in the coming months all of these documents—from SBAC and/or PARCC, and the "Publishers' Criteria." Yet none of them prescribes exactly what *curriculum* should be or how educators should implement it. That is where Rigorous Curriculum Design can play a vital role.

RCD—A Flexible Framework

The framework of Rigorous Curriculum Design is not dependent upon or tilted toward any particular commercial program or set of recommended instructional materials. It is a *flexible framework* into which quality resources can be inserted by those who should be front and center in the curriculum development decision-making process—educators and resource specialists who are valued and respected for their content expertise. The chief benefit of the RCD model is that educators can use their collective experience and insights to design the units of study *themselves*, as opposed to relying upon any commercial program—no matter how excellent it may be—to do so.

Even though selection by the curriculum design teams of the most appropriate instructional materials and resources is one of the twelve unit design steps, this selection *follows*, not precedes or takes the place of, creation of the unit "architecture" itself; that is the sole domain of the educators/designers involved. In Larry's efforts to communicate this unit design approach to others, he wrote the following core messages of the Rigorous Curriculum Design model. Note the italicized phrases in these statements; they underscore the important benefits of this educator-centered process.

Rigorous Curriculum Design Core Messages

1. The Rigorous Curriculum Design model is a *comprehensive framework that intentionally aligns* standards, assessment, instruction, curriculum, and data analysis within each unit of study.

2. The RCD model is The Leadership and Learning Center's *recommended structure* for effectively developing curricula to meet the rigor of the Common Core State Standards.

3. RCD units of study are intentionally designed to (1) *prepare students for success* on the national assessments now being developed by PARCC and SBAC and (2) ultimately fulfill the promise of the Common Core—college and career readiness for all students.

4. Rather than spend precious district funds solely on commercial programs "aligned to the Common Core," The Center instead believes in districts *investing those same funds in their educators and leaders.* When educators and leaders tap their own knowledge, skills, expertise, and experience to create the curricula they themselves will implement in their own schools, this fosters a *strong sense of professional pride and shared ownership* in the process and in the resulting products.

5. One of the great benefits of the Rigorous Curriculum Design process is its *flexibility.* It provides a recommended "roadmap" that school systems can customize to closely meet their needs and preferences, *not a rigid or prescriptive procedure* that allows for no variation or modification.

The RCD Framework at a Glance

The Rigorous Curriculum Design framework is a clearly laid out, step-by-step process that is welcomed by educators for its linearity. It begins with five foundational steps that need to take place *before* design teams develop each unit of study for a particular grade level or course. The titles of the five foundational steps and twelve unit design steps follow. Readers may wish to refer to Appendix A, which provides a paragraph description of each of these steps. *Rigorous Curriculum Design* (Ainsworth, 2010) provides a full chapter describing each step in detail along with related examples.

Foundational Steps Applicable to Each Grade and Course:

1. Prioritize the Common Core State Standards.

2. Name the Units of Study.

3. Assign the Standards—Priority and Supporting—to the Units of Study.

4. Prepare a Yearlong Pacing Calendar.

5. Create the Unit Planning Organizer.

Unit Design Steps Applied to Each Unit of Study:

1. "Unwrap" the Unit Priority Standards.

2. Create a Graphic Organizer.

3. Decide the Big Ideas and Essential Questions.

4. Create the End-of-Unit Assessment.

5. Create the Unit Pre-Assessment.

6. Identify Additional Vocabulary Terms, Interdisciplinary Connections, and 21st-Century Learning Skills.

7. Plan Engaging Learning Experiences (Authentic Performance Tasks).

8. Gather Instructional Resource Materials.

9. Recommend Effective Instruction, Differentiation, Intervention, Special Education, and English Language Learner Strategies.

10. Detail the Unit Planning Organizer.

11. Create Informal Progress-Monitoring Checks.

12. Write the Weekly Plan and Design the Daily Lessons.

The Need for Quality Curricular Units

As the number of school systems applying the RCD model to the redesign of curricula continues to multiply, we at The Leadership and Learning Center continue to receive requests for sample curricular units of study from those who have already begun developing them. Even though we *want* to share what other districts have produced, most of these units remain "in process," simply because the creation and revision of quality units often takes place over a period of months. Understandably, curriculum design teams do not want their work officially shared or published until the units of study meet their own standards of quality and excellence, and this takes time.

While fully engaged in the stimulating process of creating units of study, sometimes educators express the wistful yearning that they could—just for a while—close schools so as to be able to continue working collaboratively without interruption. The reality of education—and indeed of life itself!—is that we all have to *make time* for anything else that goes above and beyond the regular demands of each day. For educators, this means making time for the redesign of their curricula while simultaneously attending to their primary business—teaching students. To this point, we often share with audiences who have gathered to implement the RCD process a video showing a commercial airliner being completely redesigned by workers *during a flight*, with passengers and flight attendants on board, carrying on as if none of this reconstruction were happening all around them. It's a telling metaphor for our situation in education.

Since we cannot grant uninterrupted time for curriculum designers to work, what assistance can we offer? Guidance in evaluating the *quality* of their units of study. Design teams have often requested an objective set of criteria they can use to evaluate their unit products. The Rigorous Curriculum Design Unit Development Guide 1.0 provides this set of criteria. Referencing the descriptors of needed elements and quality related to each of the steps in the RCD process, design teams can identify where they need to make revisions to their initial units of study. In conducting this exercise of design team and/or peer review with follow-up revisions, they will experience an increase in confidence that what they are designing will be truly excellent and worthy of sharing with others. The RCD Unit Development Guide 1.0 appears in Appendix B. It is followed by one additional tool for evaluating each end-of-unit assessment, "Evaluating Items for Alignment, Frequency, and Quality," provided in Appendix C.

A Vision on the Near Horizon

Now more than ever, with personnel, time, and resources stretched thinner than most any of us can remember them being, we need to "work smarter, not harder" by not having to reinvent the proverbial wheel. As (nearly) an entire nation working from a common set of standards, we now have the unique opportunity to "share the wealth" of what curriculum design teams are creating within their own districts—a "common" wealth that will be applicable to almost everyone in K–12 American education.

To that end, let us all work together to share units of study that have been vetted for quality using the RCD Unit Development Guide. The primary motive behind this vision is to help and support our nation's educators by making available to them a veritable treasure trove of exemplary units of study created by their peers.

This "bank" of RCD units of study will be of most value *after* curriculum design teams have already experienced the RCD process and created their own first-draft units. Why? Every step in the process is connected to every other step. Understanding each step from *firsthand experience*—both the why and the how—will enable educators to view and use units of study *created by others* far more effectively because they will better understand the thinking that went into the creation of each one.

District Chapters

In the following chapters, you will read about how districts are successfully implementing the RCD process to redesign their curricula to fulfill the promise of the Common Core and prepare students for success on the coming national assessments. Each chapter has its own voice and stands on its own. One or more of these individual district stories of implementation may be more applicable to your situation and context than others. Yet taken collectively, these narratives provide "collective wisdom"— insights and ideas to enrich and expand us all toward understandings we may not have yet come to on our own.

CHAPTER ONE

Bloomfield Public Schools, Bloomfield, Connecticut

"During a May 2012 classroom visit, one grade 7 student revealed the depth to which RCD has now permeated our vocabulary. The student asked, 'What will be used to decide who goes to summer school, the [district] benchmark assessments or the CFAs [Common Formative Assessments]?' To this end, it is critical that all members of the educational community recognize the connections between curriculum, instruction, and assessment as they relate to the learning needs of every child, every day, in every classroom."

ELLEN STOLTZ

RCD District: Bloomfield Public Schools

Location: Bloomfield, Connecticut
(Suburban)

Population: 2,200 students

Author: Ellen Stoltz, Chief Academic Officer,
Office of Instructional Leadership

Who We Are

The suburban town of Bloomfield is located just north of the capital city of Hartford, Connecticut. Set amid rolling hills and a well-treed landscape, Bloomfield is noted for its large insurance companies, newly built churches, three PGA golf courses within the town's 26 square miles, and for the diversity of its population in race, age, and socioeconomics. In 1970, Bloomfield attained national recognition as an All-American City partly because of its racial and ethnic diversity. Today, the town of now 20,626 residents (U.S. Census, 2009) is home to African Americans, West Indians, whites, Native Americans, Asians, Indians, Pacific Islanders, and a growing population of Hispanics and Latinos. With a variety of cultural and civic offerings, and convenient access to the highway and bus line, Bloomfield offers residents a small-city character within a rural setting.

The school district serves approximately 2,200 students, with a 95 percent minority population, in contrast to the town demographic of 54 percent minority. The age categories of Bloomfield's population are equally apportioned among those under 18, 25–44, 45–64, and 65 and older, with approximately 22 percent of the total population distributed across every age range. The exception to this distribution appears in the 5.8 percent of residents who are between the ages of 18 and 24, indicating that young adults leave the town to pursue post-secondary careers and education. One little-known fact about Bloomfield is its high level of formal education relative to its population. A median household income of $53,812 enables many families to afford the predominantly single-family homes of Bloomfield to raise and educate their children.

All seven schools comprising the Bloomfield Public Schools have been renovated within the past three years to include wireless technology and interactive whiteboards in every classroom. With five neighborhood schools and two magnet schools, each school serves a targeted grade range. For example, all students enrolled in grades 3 and 4 attend Metacomet Elementary School, whereas all students enrolled in grades 7 and 8 attend Carmen Arace Middle School. The small classroom student-teacher ratio of 17:1 is another little-known fact about Bloomfield.

The Problem

In contrast to the beautiful town and school facilities, the reputation of the Bloomfield Public Schools began to suffer for two reasons:

- The perception that bright students flee to regional magnet schools because Bloomfield Public Schools do not offer a challenging curriculum;

- The reality of falling student achievement attributed to low expectations and an undemanding curriculum.

Discussions with parents and community members turn often to the topic of the lack of rigor in the existing curriculum. Comments on the status of the Bloomfield Schools made at the January 2012 stakeholders meeting represent the broader public perception of what is wrong with our schools from the community perspective. The following opinions were recorded during the meeting:

- "Curriculum is not aligned, and it's old";
- "Our classrooms do not have set expectations. We need to define high expectations for our students";
- "If staff is not requiring high expectations then students will not rise to the high expectations";
- "We need to have a curriculum that competes with state and national standards."

Parents expressed their lack of confidence in the public schools by collectively enrolling nearly 300 Bloomfield children in regional magnet, charter, private, and non-public schools.

Validating the Problem: What Does the Data Tell Us?

Achievement data collected over six years confirmed the reality that performance on the Connecticut Mastery Test (CMT) had declined in 2005–2009 and improved only marginally in 2010. For example, achievement data revealed improvement in 2006/07 on the Connecticut Academic Performance Test (CAPT) for students in grade 10 in contrast to the inconsistent gains in subsequent years. As indicated in Figures 1.1 and 1.2, academic competency for the students fell significantly below state expectations. In fact, to move toward closing the achievement gap between the state and the school district, the percentage of students scoring at competitive levels needed to be increased between 12 and 18 percent over a three-year period.

If Bloomfield Public Schools wanted to raise achievement and close the gap, then our work had to begin with redesigning the expectations and challenge of the current curriculum.

FIGURE 1.1   Overall Percentage Reading Proficient or Above: CMT

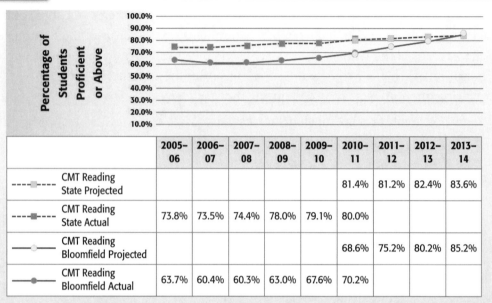

	2005–06	2006–07	2007–08	2008–09	2009–10	2010–11	2011–12	2012–13	2013–14
CMT Reading State Projected						81.4%	81.2%	82.4%	83.6%
CMT Reading State Actual	73.8%	73.5%	74.4%	78.0%	79.1%	80.0%			
CMT Reading Bloomfield Projected						68.6%	75.2%	80.2%	85.2%
CMT Reading Bloomfield Actual	63.7%	60.4%	60.3%	63.0%	67.6%	70.2%			

FIGURE 1.2   Overall Percentage Reading Proficient or Above: CAPT

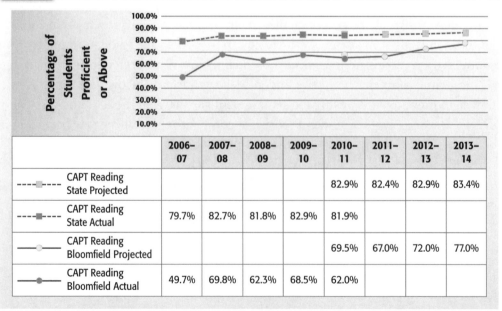

	2006–07	2007–08	2008–09	2009–10	2010–11	2011–12	2012–13	2013–14
CAPT Reading State Projected					82.9%	82.4%	82.9%	83.4%
CAPT Reading State Actual	79.7%	82.7%	81.8%	82.9%	81.9%			
CAPT Reading Bloomfield Projected					69.5%	67.0%	72.0%	77.0%
CAPT Reading Bloomfield Actual	49.7%	69.8%	62.3%	68.5%	62.0%			

How We Started

On April 4, 2011, Dr. James Thompson commenced his tenure as superintendent of the Bloomfield Public Schools. With data and research-based practices in hand and mind, Bloomfield's new educational leader expressed a consistent message to teachers, families, and principals: all adults are accountable to raise student achievement. Central to the message was the belief expressed by Vince Lombardi: "The only place that success comes before work is in the dictionary." We all knew Bloomfield Public Schools would be well positioned to meet much higher standards with sufficient and appropriate resources; a research-based plan of professional development targeting curriculum, instruction, assessment, leadership, and parent engagement for all staff; and a laser-like focus on the academic performance of every student in every classroom.

To correct the problem of low student achievement, Dr. Thompson and the new leadership team jump-started the process to meet higher standards by:

- Identifying our stakeholders and their needs, perceptions, and hopes for Bloomfield schools;

- Creating the District Accountability Plan (DAP) to match the expectations of stakeholders;

- Prioritizing the goals of the DAP to attain high academic achievement by setting targets to close the achievement gap;

- Establishing "Powerful Practices," a yearlong series of intensive professional development geared toward using standards and data to inform instruction;

- Selecting Rigorous Curriculum Design from "Powerful Practices" as the model to increase rigor of the K–12 English language arts and mathematics curriculum.

To demonstrate the need for a new curriculum design when the current curriculum had just been revised in school year 2009/10, it was the work of the leadership team to show that the curriculum's lack of rigor was associated with low expectations and poor student achievement. Conversations with Bloomfield teachers mirrored the perception that Bloomfield had experienced "bright flight" due to the number of local magnet schools. This perception fed the expectation that students came to school ill-equipped to master even the existing curriculum. To combat the perception of bright flight, the leadership team initiated a series of presentations to the board of education, PTOs, and community organizations offering data to authenticate the reality. The scatter plot in Figure 1.3 represents the actual achievement levels from the CMT for students who left the district for magnet schools.

Bloomfield Student Reading Performance on 2011 6th-Grade CMT for Currently Enrolled and No-Longer-Enrolled Students

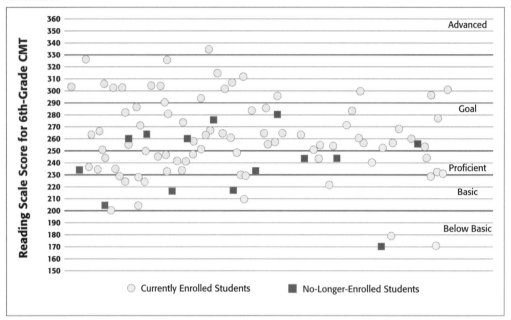

As the data revealed, the 14 students who left the district to attend a magnet school represented four of the five achievement levels, with no students leaving from the "advanced" level of performance. In fact, far more students achieving the highest levels of CMT performance continue their education as students of Bloomfield Public Schools. When this information was presented to staff and parents, the need to raise the rigor of the curricula and the expectations of our students became clear.

The Existing Curricula

Bloomfield Public Schools redesigned the K–12 English language arts (ELA) and mathematics curricula in 2010 and 2009, respectively. A review of the four-and-a-half-inch binders reveals the framework of a curriculum that includes the Connecticut State Standards, Grade-Level Expectations (GLEs), Essential Questions, materials, and resources for each unit. From a more contemporary definition of curriculum as the roadmap for what and how content standards are taught and mastered by students, the current curriculum fell short.

Now that teachers and administrators recognized the inadequacy of the current curriculum, it was easy to assess what was needed. A gap analysis of the curriculum resulted in identifying critical components of a comprehensive and challenging curriculum *not* evident in the current curriculum:

1. Prioritized standards for grade-level focus

2. Vertical alignment among and between grade levels and schools

3. Defined units of study

4. Timelines for uniform implementation

5. Overarching themes and integration of fiction and nonfiction

6. Common formative assessments aligned to prioritized standards

7. Additional learning time for reteaching or enrichment

8. Effective teaching strategies embedded in the curriculum.

It was clear to the members of the "Powerful Practices" cohort that the design of the current curriculum was now serving as the frame upon which the schools needed to build greater rigor and depth of understanding. The elements that were missing in the existing curriculum were clearly articulated in *Rigorous Curriculum Design* (Ainsworth, 2010). As a result, the Bloomfield Public Schools selected the RCD curriculum model to increase the challenge for our students and to raise student achievement. During one "Powerful Practices" workshop, a high school math teacher declared, "I have never even spoken to an elementary teacher about when problem-solving was taught in the lower grades. Now I am talking about what standards are the priority in grade 3 that align with my algebra class!"

The Bloomfield Public Schools leadership team implemented RCD, a key lever in closing the achievement gap, by:

• Providing professional development to embed research-based effective teaching strategies in all classrooms;

• Providing professional development to teachers and administrators to use Data Teams as a structure to examine student performance as part of our holistic accountability;

• Implementing and monitoring a system of benchmark assessment analysis to adjust classroom instruction as a system of holistic accountability;

• Defining and aligning research-based reading and writing strategies critical to improving comprehension;

• Implementing standards-based practices through professional learning communities (PLCs) in English language arts, professional development, and science.

While there is still much work to be done, the foundation for the accelerated transformation of our schools through curriculum redesign has been established in this transitional year.

Where We Are Today

After completing year one of "Powerful Practices," Bloomfield Public Schools initiated a 14-month process to redesign the K–12 ELA and mathematics curricula to fully align with the Common Core State Standards and the expectations of the Smarter Balanced Assessment Consortium (SBAC). With five months of targeted professional development using RCD to prioritize and "unwrap" the standards and to develop common formative assessments, the redesign process commenced March 29, 2012, with an hour-long informational meeting outlining expectations and timelines. Initially, 19 "Powerful Practices" members signed up to attend, but 38 potential curriculum redesigners streamed into the board of education conference room, including instructional coaches, classroom teachers, reading teachers, and school-based administrators.

At the initial meeting, the teams examined the RCD template adapted by the Connecticut State Department of Education and augmented by Bloomfield Public Schools. Each participant received a copy of *Rigorous Curriculum Design: How to Create Curricular Units of Study that Align Standards, Instruction, and Assessment* (Ainsworth, 2010), its companion volume, *Planning for Rigorous Curriculum Design*, the actual curriculum-writing template, and electronic links to the Common Core State Standards and curriculum-writing tools uploaded to the district Web site (www.bloomfieldschools.org). In addition, a brief, well-received presentation on integrating interactive whiteboards (IWBs) into units of study was embedded in the informational session.

The informational session ended with participants signing up for grade-level curriculum-writing teams. The grade levels of focus were: K, 2, 4, 6, 8, 9, and 10. These grades were prioritized to ensure that, upon completion of each "even" grade, the grade-level content and requisite skills would be vertically aligned with that of the grade above and grade below. As the Bloomfield Public Schools are configured by grade bands (i.e., all students in grades 3 and 4 attend Metacomet Elementary School), it is critical that the redesigned curricula connect from grade to grade (and school to school) what students need to know and be able to do in ELA and mathematics. Notably, grade 9 was also included on the recommendation of the assistant principal of Bloomfield High School, due to the district- and school-wide focus on improving literacy for freshman students. As a result, all school sites have staff represented and actively participating in the redesign.

Two large-group meetings were held at strategic times during the remainder of the 2011/12 school year. The April 26, 2012, meeting provided each team enough time to scrutinize the specific elements of the grade 6 ELA units of study to ensure all redesign teams understood the task. The "interdisciplinary concept map" was also introduced as a schema for creating interdisciplinary connections based in linking fiction and nonfiction from ELA to science and social studies. The June 14 meeting allocated time for redesign teams to showcase their work to the larger group. Both meetings served as important levers for the groups to develop both the conceptual and practical knowledge of the work ahead.

After six weeks of dedicated small-group work, the drafts are nearing completion for at least one unit of study per grade level. All units of study are uploaded into grade-level folders on our protected shared drive, enabling accessibility to all templates for all curriculum redesign teams. While teachers are taking a break from curriculum writing between July 1 and August 27, the chief academic officer will review and provide feedback to teams on the work completed as of June 30, 2012.

Where We Are Going

The May 2012 District Accountability Plan (DAP) guides our decisions and subsequent actions to improve the district and to hold all adults accountable for progress. The plan describes four priorities that will lead to the realization of our vision, one of which is as follows:

> *"We will redesign and strengthen the district's curriculum, instruction, and assessment to align with the rigor of Connecticut's Common Core State Standards in reading and math."*

The DAP lists the action steps the curriculum redesign teams will take:

1. Analyze gaps within the current curriculum and align with Common Core State Standards.

2. Identify standards-based themes and interdisciplinary connections.

3. Identify Big Ideas and Essential Questions.

4. Connect interdisciplinary comprehension strategies and levels of questioning.

5. Design instructional plans in electronic, accessible form.

6. Update common formative assessments and create authentic performance tasks to align with Common Core State Standards.

7. Align content pacing schedule with CMT and CAPT.

8. Construct standards-based report cards.

9. Implement feedback mechanisms, such as walkthrough protocols, academic review, and lesson study to support instructional improvement and to adjust curriculum.

RCD creator Larry Ainsworth will lead our August 28–29, 2012, RCD workshop with a focus on aligning RCD and the CCSS to the development of common formative assessments and to the even more demanding authentic performance tasks. Larry will work directly with each of the six teams, offering feedback on the draft units of study. Our goal is to "test-drive" one ELA unit in Fall 2012, with a follow-up large-group session in mid-September for reflection on its success. Although the timeline to complete the fully redesigned curricula for ELA and mathematics is June 30, 2013, the curricula will live on the school's password-protected Web site in electronic form, enabling teachers to contribute and revise as units of study are implemented.

How We Will Know We Are Successful

Bloomfield's three-year goal is to increase the percentage of teachers who implement with fidelity a standards-based curriculum aligned to the Common Core State Standards. Our key strategy is to redesign all curriculum, instruction, and assessment practices to align with the rigor of the Common Core and to be informed by the results of common formative assessments and authentic performance tasks. Measurement of the percentage of teachers who implement RCD with fidelity will occur through the new teacher evaluation system.

The effectiveness of the new curriculum will be monitored by field-testing lesson plans and assessments in our classrooms within the established time frame of school year 2012/13. As we complete each action step, a progress report will be disseminated to teachers and will be posted on the Bloomfield Public Schools Web site. The target date for completion of the English language arts and mathematics curricula is July 2013. The target date for full implementation is September 2013.

First, curriculum redesign teams will align curriculum, instruction, and assessment in grades K–12 to the Common Core State Standards. Field-testing units of study will be one indicator of successful completion of the new curriculum as teachers and students actually try out the Big Ideas, levels of questioning, CFAs, and performance tasks. Second, the new teacher evaluation system will link curriculum to instructional delivery via lesson planning and monitoring for understanding, ensuring all teachers use the curriculum effectively. Principals and teachers will use the new design and provide feedback to the curriculum redesign teams.

What does this look like? In every classroom, effective instruction targets the learning outcomes students need to master in reading and math. Regularly scheduled tests, called Benchmark Cycle Assessments, in combination with more frequent CFAs, enable us to see where students have mastered material and where we need to provide additional learning support. The results of the assessments guide each Data Team to pinpoint the questions to ask and the skills to practice in reading and math. Mapping the curriculum and planning the time frame to implement the units of study allots a "reinforcing week" immediately following each unit. During this time, students receive differentiated instruction and support based on their specific learning needs. Targeted instruction focuses on the strategies required to advance learning to the next level.

Positive Change Already

Bloomfield's district leadership, principals, teachers, parents, and stakeholders all share in the same goal: the success of our students. With our willingness to work tirelessly to meet our goal, it has been our belief this school year that success will come *after work* where it is most important—in our efforts as educators and in the achievement of our children. The work began in April 2011 with the creation of a comprehensive plan to transform the school system from a record of underperformance to one of competitive achievement. With the RCD process already in place for the "Powerful Practices" cohort, every teacher in the district was invited to prioritize the K–12 ELA and math standards in September 2011 and received customized flipbooks with their selected standards highlighted to showcase their input from the September workshop. The focus on teaching to the standards listed in the flipbooks accelerated the vertical alignment and increased the rigor we needed.

On the evening of July 8, 2012, the leadership team was the first to view the secure state-embargoed performance data for Bloomfield Public Schools. The *Hartford Courant* posted the gains on July 17, stating "The number of high school students scoring at or above the state goal increased by 8.2 percentage points in math and 16.4 percentage points in reading." Also noteworthy, "Third grade students scoring at or above the state goal increased from 39.4 percent to 51.8 percent." How did this dramatic change occur? In combination with Data Teams at every level of the school and district, instruction was focused on the prioritized standards in reading and math.

The initial results of our annual high-stakes assessments are now a measure of the progress made toward our goals for our students, our schools, and our town. Using formative data to inform instruction based on standards prioritized by colleagues is truly a formula for success. One important quote underscores this point: "Assessment must be seen as an instructional tool for use while learning is occurring, and as an accountability tool to determine if learning has occurred" (NEA, 2003).

We are seeing this quote in action in our schools. During a May 2012 classroom visit, one grade 7 student revealed the depth to which RCD has now permeated our vocabulary. The student asked, "What will be used to decide who goes to summer school, the [district] benchmark assessments or the CFAs?" To this end, it is critical that all members of the educational community recognize the connections between curriculum, instruction, and assessment as they relate to the learning needs of every child, every day, in every classroom.

What's Next?

As we approach the upcoming 2012/13 school year, the redesign teams will create more rigorous curricula using the RCD template in combination with the Bloomfield universal lesson design. The draft teacher evaluation system aligns with the observable components of the curriculum to ensure the curriculum will be monitored and implemented with fidelity. Teachers will be vetting the units of study, creating sample questions referencing Bloom's taxonomy and Webb's Depth of Knowledge (DOK), and selecting electronic instructional resources and materials for classrooms. Parents will be informed of the prioritized standards their children need to know and be able to do as the redesign team subcommittee develops new standards-based report cards and progress reports.

The successful educators in Bloomfield Public Schools are invested in the collaborative work that must be done to ensure that all students in our charge have a bright future ahead of them. Teachers have shown the willingness to learn and grow right along with our students. Administrators and teachers are embracing the positive changes in the spirit of professional self-improvement and have done so with enthusiasm and focus. Aligned with the superintendent's original message, all adults see the connection between their actions and the resulting level of student achievement. In the words of Dr. Thompson, "Success will come *after work* where it is most important—in our efforts as educators and in the achievement of our children."

Getting Started on Your Journey

As you reflect on the Bloomfield School District's experience, think about how their story applies to you in your current setting, and then answer the following questions:

1. As evidenced early on in the chapter, the district went through an in-depth needs analysis to determine where their curriculum was missing the mark:

   > Now that teachers and administrators recognized the inadequacy of the current curriculum, it was easy to assess what was needed. A gap analysis of the curriculum resulted in identifying critical components of a comprehensive and challenging curriculum **not** evident in our current curriculum:
   >
   > - Prioritized standards for grade-level focus;
   > - Vertical alignment among and between grade levels and schools;
   > - Defined units of study;
   > - Timelines for uniform implementation;
   > - Overarching themes and integration of fiction and nonfiction;
   > - Common formative assessments aligned to prioritized standards;
   > - Additional learning time for reteaching or enrichment;
   > - Effective teaching strategies embedded in the curriculum.

   a. Has your school or district been through this, or a similar type of process, to ascertain the strengths and weaknesses of your current curriculum? Explain.

   b. Looking at the eight areas Bloomfield identified as "needs improvement," many of these are essential building blocks of the Rigorous Curriculum Design model. Take a moment to reflect upon what components are your strengths and which ones are opportunities for growth in your setting. Place a star next to those elements that are most critical for your school or district to work on, and then establish at least one action item that will ensure you revisit this conversation with necessary stakeholders.

2. *During one "Powerful Practices" workshop, a high school math teacher declared, "I have never even spoken to an elementary teacher about when problem-solving was taught in the lower grades. Now I am talking about what standards are the priority in grade 3 that align with my algebra class!"*

Does this type of vertical alignment exist in your setting? Why or why not?

CHAPTER TWO

Anaheim City School District, Orange County, California

"Without argument, however, the most impressive outcome was the impact of Rigorous Curriculum Design on our students during the pilot. Feedback from the committee members during the initial pilot was overwhelmingly positive. They were excited and a little surprised by the level of enthusiasm and passion for learning demonstrated by their students during the units. Teachers began the units with lots of apprehension and concern that the tasks would be too difficult. Instead, multiple stories were related of struggling students who were able to demonstrate high levels of success within the collaborative, authentic, and highly motivating structure of the units."

MARY O'NEIL GRACE

"The Common Core standards and the development of specific units have given our district the opportunity to have greater teacher and student engagement. Teachers collaborated in the writing of the units, and students played a role in piloting and testing in each unit to check for effectiveness. I believe that the units will allow for creative flexibility for our teachers and students, and therefore will better prepare students to be independent, innovative thinkers ready to take on the 21st-century world."

SUE PRUES,
ANAHEIM CITY SCHOOL DISTRICT, BOARD PRESIDENT

RCD District: Anaheim City School District

Location: Orange County, California
(Urban)

Population: 21,000+ students

Author: Mary O'Neil Grace, Ed.D., Assistant
Superintendent, Education Services

District Information

Anaheim City School District (ACSD) is located in Orange County, California, and provides educational services to more than 21,000 students at 24 K–6 schools. Five schools are on a year-round, multitrack calendar and 19 schools are on a modified single-track calendar. The percentage of Hispanic students continues to grow while the percentages of African American and white students have declined. Remaining fairly constant is the percentage of students of Asian, Pacific Islander, and Philippine descent. In ACSD, the major ethnic populations include 85.5 percent Hispanic/Latino, 5.1 percent white (not Hispanic), 4.7 percent Asian, 1.7 percent African American, and 1.6 percent Filipino. Of these students' primary languages, 75 percent speak Spanish, 19 percent speak English, 2 percent speak Vietnamese, and 4 percent speak other languages. Ten percent of all students in the district are eligible for CalWORKs, and 85.5 percent are eligible for free or reduced-priced lunches. Of the district's 1,046 classroom teachers, 98.2 percent are fully credentialed (1.2 percent are emergency credentialed).

The ACSD Board of Education has guiding principles that include the following:

- Ensuring students receive a well-rounded, holistic education that includes core academic curriculum consisting of literacy, numeracy, social and scientific studies, visual and performing arts/music, bilingualism, technological competency, and information literacy;

- Ensuring students exit our K–6 system with their creativity maximized and as strong problem solvers and critical thinkers.

Since 2003, we have utilized the same English language arts curriculum. In 2003, 15 of our schools began implementation of Reading First, a federal grant that focused on providing professional development in language arts that included curriculum implementation, data analysis, and fidelity to the program. Through the Reading First grant, our district developed a consistent understanding and use of the adopted curriculum. However, we did not have a common understanding of the standards and whether or not the standards and the curriculum were aligned. In 2008, a district-wide committee was formed to identify and pace the California Content Standards in reading, writing, and math. While the district vision was for all teachers to know, understand, and utilize the identified Power Standards (prioritized, grade-specific *state* standards determined to be essential for student understanding and readiness for the next level of learning), we did not provide the appropriate professional development and support for full implementation. Through school visits we ultimately realized that there were schools where the standards were the curriculum and the textbooks were the tools, and others that showed evidence that standards were not being utilized. With the adoption of the Common Core State Standards, we decided to formulate a plan to ensure alignment of the standards—written, taught, and assessed.

The Implementation Process

Our journey into Rigorous Curriculum Design (RCD) began in June of 2011 with an orientation for administrators delivered by The Leadership and Learning Center and with the selection of committee members. We asked principals to recommend teachers from their respective school sites based on Larry Ainsworth's professional characteristic recommendations: belief in the work, experience in teaching, work ethic, commitment to the project, strong interpersonal skills, willingness to take risks, flexibility, and attention to detail. The RCD Committee in Anaheim City School District would be comprised of general education teachers from each grade level, and special day class, resource specialist, gifted and talented, and dual immersion teachers. Our main goal was to have a committee representative of all 24 school sites and all teaching roles, and balanced between the primary and upper grades. We felt strongly about the process being teacher-driven, so a secondary goal in committee formation was to develop experts at each school site. Additionally, curriculum coaches, principals, curriculum specialists, and parents were included in our 80-member committee.

During the summer of 2011 we conferenced with the team from The Leadership and Learning Center to secure nine professional development dates for the 2011/12 school year. As an elementary school district, that meant we needed to contract for days when we were able to secure substitute teachers for the 60 classroom teachers on the committee. The decision was made to use the RCD model with the newly adopted Common Core State Standards, adding a few layers for which we would need additional support. Through multiple conversations with our Center consultant, Paul Bloomberg, we were able to map out a logical progression of professional development sessions that met the needs and priorities of our district.

As our single-track school sites returned in September, we were excited to begin working with Paul and The Leadership and Learning Center. The first step was to present the RCD model for the full committee, as well as an overview of the English language arts Common Core State Standards. Both of these concepts were new to the 80 members of the committee. As a system, Anaheim City School District was still moving away from a strong reliance on program curricula and had limited experience in unit development. Additionally, many people in the room were just becoming aware of the Common Core State Standards Initiative. By the end of day two, our committee members left the room with overwhelmed expressions on their faces. However, as we spoke to them they assured us they were excited and enthusiastic about the prospects ahead.

In early October, we dove into the foundational stages of building our units. In three full-day sessions, with Paul's guidance, the committee reached consensus on a common set of prioritized, kindergarten through sixth-grade English language arts Common Core standards. Each grade level made initial attempts at placing those standards into units and started the "unwrapping," or deconstruction, of Common Core standards process. The fact that ACSD had used Larry Ainsworth's system of selecting Power (Priority) Standards for the 1997 California State Standards was definitely to our advantage. Several committee members had been part of that process, either at a school site or district level; all committee members were familiar with the selection and implementation of Power Priority Standards.

This foundational stage proved to be one of the most important steps in our journey. Our committee members began to feel as if they were part of something powerful and were proud of the decisions they made for the district as a whole. We also realized that using the RCD process to prepare for the Common Core State Standards gave an authentic relevance to the project. Our committee members recognized a need and were motivated to put forth the effort to develop a product to meet that need.

Over a series of four more professional development days, we were trained in the modules dedicated to common formative assessments and authentic performance tasks. Working through these topics proved to be demanding in that each day was filled with new learning. The committee relied on the expert guidance from our consultant to challenge our practices and lead us toward powerful possibilities. Specifically, the common formative assessment module provided the rationale to move from exclusive multiple-choice assessments to varied assessment formats. With our district's high population of English language learners, we were well aware of the limitations multiple-choice assessments create for our students; however, under the No Child Left Behind model of assessments, changes had not yet been made. While research has long supported the use of brief, targeted, collaboratively created assessments to drive instruction and provide students with clear feedback, the Common Core initiative and next-generation assessment specifications sparked more teacher buy-in and gave us reasons for making the change.

Another ACSD practice that was challenged during these modules was our implementation of direct instruction lessons. We had previously invested a significant amount of time and energy training our teachers within the direct instruction method; but our general implementation often resulted in explicit lessons at a basic level of rigor. One of our greatest challenges, as a whole system, was transferring control of the learning to students through a gradual release of responsibility. Many teachers moved from one modeled lesson to another with limited opportunities for students to apply their understandings of the standards. Our teachers were working diligently but not always seeing the results they hoped for with their students. Adding the layer of authentic performance tasks to initial lessons taught through the direct instruction model was a perfect match.

About midyear we faced another challenge: a revision of our initial goal. Initially, our plan was to have the committee write a year's worth of units for each grade level by June of 2012. At this point, we realized the accuracy of Larry Ainsworth's assertion that this is a multiyear process. It really does take multiple years! Our resulting decision to focus on developing reading and writing units for just one six-week time period seemed to be much more manageable. It also brought much relief to Paul Bloomberg, who had questioned our original idea from the start, especially within the constraints of training 80 people at one time.

Further reflection led to another discovery. In our attempts to reach equitability in our committee design, we learned the limits of effective collaboration. Each grade-level team consisted of 10–12 members. That number was great for idea generation, but proved to be a hindrance for reaching consensus for task completion. Some teams managed and functioned well under these constraints, while other teams literally had moments of deadlock. It was at this point, in January 2012, as our formal professional development sessions were ending, that we moved to smaller subcommittees to massage and finalize the initial unit plans.

We divided the remaining work into three separate subcommittees, which met over a series of dates in February and March. Our "vertical consistency subcommittee" reviewed representation of the standards within the units and worked through pacing guide inconsistencies. A second subcommittee focused on refinement of the common formative assessments, with a third subcommittee refining the authentic performance tasks. The smaller scale of these subcommittees allowed for a review and feedback mechanism across the seven grade levels, which led to drastic improvements in consistency as well as content. It was at this stage that student documents were developed. Looking back on the process, this was a pivotal move for those of us overseeing the process. What looked to be an impossible task in late January resulted in actual, concrete documents by the end of March.

We made preparations for an initial pilot of the units by our committee members. Critical professional development needed to occur before we could successfully pilot the units. A frequent question from our committee that remained unresolved was how our current practices would be incorporated into this new curricular model. In an additional release day, we communicated changes made by the subcommittee and also addressed the following issues:

- Illustrating where and how the direct instruction model fit within this unit design;

- Ensuring that scaffolds and supports for our English language learners continued to guarantee success for all of our students;
- Planning for gradual release of responsibility of a standard over a series of lessons that built in rigor.

In late May and early June, our committee members piloted the six-week reading and writing units. Many committee members included other teachers from their school site's grade-level team in the pilot. As we visited classroom after classroom, the enthusiasm and engagement of the students within the units was amazing. We were pleased to see the increased opportunities for students to engage in supported, oral language rehearsal of concepts and skills within the collaborative nature of the tasks. Teachers openly shared that the amount of planning required was more than they expected, but they were bursting at the seams to share success stories of low-performing students surpassing their expectations within the collaborative and authentic tasks.

Looking ahead, a small team of our committee members has taken the feedback from the pilot units and made revisions to the initial units. Next school year, all teachers will receive a one-day professional development experience to prepare them for an initial implementation of the Common Core State Standards within the RCD structure of the units. By February of 2013, all 600 teachers in the district will have engaged in a full pilot of the six-week reading and writing units and will have been encouraged to provide feedback. Additional units will continue to be developed with an expected full implementation of the English language arts Common Core standards using the RCD model anticipated for the 2013/14 school year—one year ahead of the initial roll-out of the Smarter Balanced Assessment Consortium system.

Success and Challenges

Our yearlong journey with The Leadership and Learning Center resulted in numerous benefits that made any of the struggles we encountered all the more worthwhile.

Foremost is the change that has occurred in our assessment practices. We now have a large team of teachers trained in the creation and scoring of common formative assessments. Collaborative creation of the common formative assessment items has provided our system with a level of calibration we have not experienced before. Teachers realize the benefits of utilizing varied assessment formats to truly match the intent and rigor of the standard. Most importantly, we have evidence, via our initial pilot of the units, of the power that scoring rubrics provide for student feedback and resulting success.

In our opinion, another important benefit is that this process challenged our system to reflect on and improve our instructional practices. The Common Core State

Standards will continue to be introduced in our district utilizing the Explicit Direct Instruction model (Hollingsworth and Ybarra, 2009) with scaffolds for English language learners and other research-based strategies. However, instead of focusing on designing individual lessons, the format of the authentic performance tasks has provided support in envisioning purposeful, gradual release of responsibility of learning to our students over a series of lessons. This process has allowed us to plan for a series of related lessons beginning with initial understanding of concepts and skills, leading toward true, authentic application of the standards within each performance task.

Without argument, however, the most impressive outcome was the impact of Rigorous Curriculum Design on our students during the pilot. Feedback from the committee members during the initial pilot was overwhelmingly positive. They were excited and a little surprised by the level of enthusiasm and passion for learning demonstrated by their students during the units. Teachers began the units with lots of apprehension and concern that the tasks would be too difficult. Instead, multiple stories were related of struggling students who were able to demonstrate high levels of success within the collaborative, authentic, and highly motivating structure of the units.

Such successes have seemed to rejuvenate our committee members as we look toward the challenges that remain. Taking this process to all teachers and developing remaining units still seems quite daunting.

Between July and December of 2012, we will provide multiple one-day trainings for all 600 teachers in our district. The trainings will address an overview of the English language arts Common Core standards, orientation to the RCD model, and familiarity with the reading and writing units of study, as well as issues related to changes to our current planning practices. We are encouraged by the number of teachers who are voluntarily attending summer sessions of this professional development. Having such a large number of invested and trained committee members will certainly be a definite asset. As we train the larger system, they will share stories, visuals, and video clips from the successful initial pilot.

Continued development of future units will remain a formidable challenge. At this point, reading and writing units for one six-week time span are complete. Leveraging resources and committee member availability to write five more sets of integrated reading and writing units will be a substantial undertaking. The size of our committee will be an asset. However, due to natural attrition, promotions, and movement of teachers, we are left with a smaller group from which to draw. Thus, we must also address the fact that we are now faced with two of our school sites not having representation. Leveraging the success from the pilot to provide the initial motivation as well as the belief that the process will become easier with each unit written will be critical.

Reflections and Expectations for the Future

As we reflect on our journey this year, it is clear that without structure and guidance from The Leadership and Learning Center, we would not have moved toward this initial implementation of the English language arts Common Core State Standards through the RCD model in such an effective or timely manner. Our consultant, Paul Bloomberg, was able to promote what was necessary for success when, at times, our committee was unable to see beyond current practices. His gentle recommendation of what he knew to be effective helped our committee find solutions to challenges. The fact that Paul had facilitated other districts' system change was very powerful. Without his prior experiences and examples, we would not have come as far as we did. The decision to begin this process with the Common Core State Standards was pivotal. As we have a new set of standards, we also have a new set of instructional practices to assist our students in accomplishing the rigor within these standards.

The best way to describe the impact of this process on our system is through comments of our committee members related to the initial pilot.

- "I think for the first two weeks I went into panic mode, but after that everything seemed to fall into place and make much more sense. Because the tasks built on themselves, it made it evident right away where students had holes and how to differentiate instruction to meet everyone's needs," said April Ortiz, primary special day class teacher. As a side note, April also shared pictures of her students, many of whom are on the autistic spectrum, successfully collaborating with one another.

- "The unit really did go well. I felt like the kids really wanted to do something rigorous even though we were at the end of the school year. They were committed to high quality as well as deep thinking," said Matthew Holland, Gifted and Talented Education (GATE), third-grade teacher.

- "Teaching the [Rigorous Curriculum Design] project opened my eyes to a new world of collaboration for students. They were eager to learn, work together, and produce high-quality work. Each task required thought-provoking questions, discussions, and teamwork to get them accomplished. It provided the pathway for ELL and Resource Specialist Program (RSP) students to feel successful and accomplished," said Julie Jones, general education, fifth-grade teacher.

- "The development of the Common Core standards and specifically the rigorous units of study are an exciting change coming to the education of our young people. For Anaheim City, this forward-thinking process aligns well with the board's vision of providing a well-rounded holistic education with high expectations for all Anaheim children," said a school board member.

- "As a school board member and university professor I am excited for our teachers, young scholars, and community overall as we move toward a curriculum that will bring the joy back to teaching *and* learning. A 21st-century education requires that our students not only develop their critical thinking, communication, creativity, and collaboration skills, but that they learn to apply those skills. Through Rigorous Curriculum Design we are modeling what we expect from our students as our educators apply their critical thinking, communication, creativity, and collaboration skills to assure our students get a rigorous, relevant, and well-rounded 21st-century education," said Dr. Jose Moreno, board member.

- "The Common Core standards and the development of specific units have given our district the opportunity to have greater teacher and student engagement. Teachers collaborated in the writing of the units, and students played a role in piloting and testing in each unit to check for effectiveness. I believe that the units will allow for creative flexibility for our teachers and students, and therefore will better prepare students to be independent, innovative thinkers ready to take on the 21st-century world," said Sue Prues, Anaheim City School District board president.

As we look to the future, our initial plan is to complete a total of six units of study following the RCD process for the California Common Core State Standards for English Language Arts and Literacy in History/Social Studies, Science, and Technical Subjects as well as continue building authentic performance tasks that require students to utilize 21st-century skills of collaboration, critical thinking and problem solving, communication, and creativity and innovation. Our district has included the Data Teams training for administrators and curriculum coaches, which will help further develop an infrastructure that will maximize the effects of the units.

In order to have a successful transition we will need to focus our vision on the teaching and learning systems around the right college and career readiness outcomes for all students. It is crucial to design curricula and assessment systems that emphasize authentic, real-world problems, engage students in inquiry and exploration, and provide opportunities for students to apply what they know in meaningful ways.

Getting Started on Your Journey

As you reflect on Anaheim City School District's methodology, think about how their story applies to you in your current setting, and then answer the following questions:

1. ACSD put a lot of thought into how they would select the educators who would serve on their Rigorous Curriculum Design pilot committee. They developed criteria for how they would be chosen and wanted to ensure representation from each of the schools. In addition, they wanted to work with educators who could be empowered to take on the work with passion:

> *We felt strongly about the process being teacher-driven, so a secondary goal in committee formation was to develop experts for each school site…. As a system, Anaheim City School District was still moving away from a strong reliance on program curricula with limited experience in unit development.*

> Who or what drives unit development and design in your district? Is it the educators, the textbook series, the pacing guides, or something else? Explain.

2. *Without argument, however, the most impressive outcome was the impact of Rigorous Curriculum Design on our students during the pilot. Feedback from the committee members during the initial pilot was overwhelmingly positive. They were excited and a little surprised by the level of enthusiasm and passion for learning demonstrated by their students during the units. Teachers began the units with lots of apprehension and concern that the tasks would be too difficult. Instead, multiple stories were related of struggling students who were able to demonstrate high levels of success within the collaborative, authentic, and highly motivating structure of the units.*

> One of the key components of the Rigorous Curriculum Design model is the inclusion of authentic performance tasks, otherwise known as performance assessment. This type of assessment model will be included in the creation of the Common Core State Standards assessments, and has been proved to give

teachers the information they need regarding student mastery of targeted concepts and skills, while at the same time infusing joy and enthusiasm for the learner.

Do you use performance tasks as a means of ensuring students are proficient in prioritized and "unwrapped" standards? If yes, what types of performance tasks do you administer? If no, what obstacles exist that get in the way of being able to utilize this powerful instruction and learning strategy?

3. It is clear throughout the chapter that while this work is highly meaningful and the right work to be about, it is also strenuous: *Working through these topics proved to be demanding in that each day was filled with new learning. The committee relied on the expert guidance from our trainer to challenge our practices and lead us toward powerful possibilities.*

No one in education would tell you they have a great deal of time on their hands—every teacher and leader is insanely busy trying to determine how to best reach and teach their learners. However, sometimes we are busy focusing on the wrong work, or the things that do not yield the results we desire. Are you currently putting your time and energy into what works best (like implementing well-designed units of study)? How do you know?

CHAPTER THREE

Raytown Quality Schools, Raytown, Missouri

"It is a shared feeling among district educators that the Common Core standards combined with Rigorous Curriculum Design will allow us to create and maintain a curriculum process and product that will stand the test of the rigorous performance assessments coming in the next two years. It is inspiring to watch what a dedicated teacher can do when given a strong curriculum, practiced techniques, and the freedom and power to innovate."

JANIE PYLE, Ed.D.,
ASSOCIATE SUPERINTENDENT

RCD District: Raytown Quality Schools

Location: Raytown, Missouri (Urban)

Population: 8,800 students

Author: Janie Pyle, Ed.D.,
Associate Superintendent

Raytown Quality Schools is an urban district of approximately 8,800 students. The City of Raytown is 10.4 square miles and is located southeast of downtown Kansas City, Missouri. Raytown Quality Schools serve a larger area of 32 square miles, with six zip codes and boundaries located within three cities. Six of our 19 schools are located within the city limits of Kansas City. We have 10 elementary schools, three middle schools, two high schools, one alternative school, one special education school for the severely handicapped, one career and technical education center, and a preschool supported by federal funds. Raytown is a very tight-knit community with a strong history and a changing demographic. Our minority student population, which has risen steadily for the last 10 years, is approximately 60 percent.

When I was hired in July of 2008 as the Associate Superintendent of Curriculum and Instruction and Personnel, the superintendent of schools gave me the directive to focus all energy into changing the direction of our test scores, which had been trending downward for several years. The Raytown demographic had been changing slowly for the past 10 years, with a steady increase in minority students, students with special needs, and families moving into the district from areas described as having failing schools. Enrollment in the district had decreased over the last six years and rental housing increased. At the same time, the attendance rate in the district was a fairly steady 94 percent, with a graduation rate of approximately 85 percent. Obviously, students were experiencing success and wanted to attend school. While the demographic changed, it was my opinion that this was not significant enough for the district to experience such sporadic scores.

The state accountability test (known as the Missouri Assessment Program, or MAP) had made adjustments in how scores were reported, which could account for some of the change in scores; however, the logical next step was to complete a thorough review of the current curriculum, including practices in instruction and assessment and the support for increased educator effectiveness across the district. I devoted significant time studying research related to curriculum, standardization, and design of instructional delivery. The two specific works of research that assisted us in our journey were *Focus* by Mike Schmoker (2011) and *Rigorous Curriculum Design* by Larry Ainsworth (2010). I contacted colleagues, asked questions of those who were experiencing success, and developed Big Ideas that shaped the vision of the task ahead.

Curriculum Needs Assessment

The purpose of this massive project was three-fold:

1. To get a full picture of the work done in and out of the classroom in support of student achievement (establish status);

2. To establish a baseline for all processes, procedures, and behaviors that impact student achievement in any way (the beginning of the data review process);

3. To recognize the work of everyone in all positions that contribute to student achievement in our district with the goal to get everyone to move "roughly west" or in the same direction for kids (the beginning of collaboration).

Process

We began in July of 2008 with what we called a "Black and White Audit" (named as a way to say "we either have what we need or we do not"). This audit is a thorough intensive review of any and all processes, procedures, policies, and events that have or could possibly have an effect on student achievement. *Rigorous Curriculum Design* calls this process the "curriculum needs assessment." This was an intensive process that took approximately four months to complete and required the collection of many materials (online and hard copy) that would assist us in discovering the state of curriculum, instruction, and support in the district: e.g., texts, supplementals, sample lesson plans, student assessments (formative and summative), student work, curriculum sources and documents, schedules, handbooks, board policies and administrative procedures, and equipment lists. A "yes" or "no" check sheet was used to inventory what materials were available, what was being used, and what was missing. Rubrics were constructed to measure the quality and level of curriculum planning and delivery.

In addition, administrator walkthrough observations were conducted at every building by the district instructional team for the purpose of experiencing actual instruction in a snapshot form. Classroom assessments and student work were collected from all teachers to make the connection between the observed instructional practices and student learning. These observations and collections were used in conjunction with student performance data and then matched to exemplars in instructional strategies and classroom assessment. Data was also collected regarding discipline to check the amount of time students were outside of the learning environment due to behavior issues. We also reviewed every instructional support program, including federal and title, gifted and talented, English language learning, special education, and other intervention programs. In addition we reviewed professional development practices, new teacher training, mentoring protocols, and other teacher supports. We conducted interviews with various staff members in all positions across the district. When we were satisfied that our study of current practices was complete, we began the process of pouring through the information looking for answers.

Audit Results

The overall results of the 2008 audit were extensive and indicated some very specific strengths in practice as well as clear indicators for change within the district. The primary strength was in the area of support.

The superintendent and board of education are highly supportive and genuinely interested in the state of education in the district. Finances are focused on student needs and on school and teacher support. Significant funding is designated for professional development, the purchase of textbooks, and in the availability and implementation of technology resources for instruction and operations. Also noted was the depth of specialized programs that support students through alternative settings, the availability of full-time curriculum and instruction coordinators, as well as personnel specific to classroom and teaching support such as librarians, counselors, social workers, and behavior interventionists. Educational options such as career education, gifted and talented and enrichment classes, and higher-education certificate programs also provide a wide safety net for just about every academic or social need that students may have.

With these powerful practices in place, it was clear that Raytown provided the support necessary to lead to student success. On the other hand, the audit also revealed that changes had to be made in the area of curriculum and instruction.

The first obvious conclusion was that curriculum was not standardized, so actual instruction and specific student expectation was difficult to address as a district, making what data we did have sporadic, unclear, and less useful. Overall, instruction seemed to lack focus on specific learning objectives tied to the state grade- and course-level expectations. Informal survey results of staff indicated that many teachers had not reviewed the state standards and no real curriculum was available to them. Classroom visits revealed that there was little common planning of material and lessons. Assessments were, for the most part, teacher-specific and did not match other assessments given by teachers in the same grade or subject. As a result, one particular grade level or content area often did not teach the same material or focus on the same learning objectives. This lack of standardization supported the fact that what data was collected in the district did not provide a clear reason for declining student achievement.

Teacher and student materials, along with observations, revealed that Raytown has a highly sophisticated staff in terms of content knowledge and they have a strong willingness to perform the task at hand. However, at the time of this audit, instruction lacked variety and rigor and tended to be presented at a lower level of performance expectation. Classroom assessments tended to match this level of instruction, requiring students to demonstrate a lower depth of knowledge (DOK). Lesson planning lacked organization, was project-based, or in some cases was not required or present.

With respect to teacher learning, prior professional development included grant-funded initiative-based programs and was effective for those who attended and followed through with the strategies and programing. However, there was limited monitoring and follow-through. As a result, the programs and strategies, however strong and researched, were not consistently used throughout the district.

When the audit was complete and the findings were shared with the staff, the response by many unveiled a readiness for change to the "what and how" of curriculum and instruction. Others were skeptical, which was to be expected. There was a great deal of freedom in planning instruction and assessment. Whatever the state of the attitudes, knowledge or skill level of the staff, it was time to move away from business as usual.

> *Solution: A need for transformation from sporadic and unclear goals and expectations to a focused, consistent set of learning targets designed for student success.*

As I had done in past school districts, I spent significant time reviewing the type, level, and expectation of assessments given by teachers during the course of their instruction. The connection of strong, well-written assessments with instruction is evident throughout the research on teaching and learning. Clearly, we needed to focus on higher student expectations for learning through the development of effective assessments designed at a higher depth of knowledge. This, in turn, would directly affect the delivery and level of instruction by the teacher. We organized articulation discussions with staff between grades and among content areas. These dialogues gave teachers a picture of the skills and knowledge that students were expected to demonstrate.

At the same time, we organized groups of teachers that reviewed and prioritized the state standards. This was long, difficult work that required trained facilitators to assist the groups as they worked through the overwhelming number of standards in each content and grade. We revamped our professional development to include overviews of effective assessment writing, classroom organization, and effective instructional strategies. It was important to provide a venue where teachers could actively participate in planning for their own learning.

As a result of this work, clearly defined Major Learner Objectives (MLOs) were created, with prioritized grade- and course-level expectations listed under each. From this information, teachers were able to identify student performance objectives and tie assessments to each objective. Units of study were developed along with pacing guides. Teachers had a venue where they could actively participate in the planning for their own learning. Administrators learned the skills needed to support these efforts and to manage their time to devote more energy to teaching and learning.

The board of education gave a specific support to the district by voting to approve "early out Wednesdays" to allow teachers to have focused professional development every Wednesday afternoon for 90 minutes. Specific teacher training time on Wednesdays kept us from having to use substitute teachers during the day or keep teachers after school for training. We now provide the necessary teacher learning *and* maintain consistent classroom instruction.

In order to support the transitions that teachers were making, I began a specific study with the administrative staff with the goal of changing the focus of the building administrator from manager to instructional leader. *Leaders of Learning* (2011), by Richard Dufour and Robert Marzano, speaks specifically about the relationship between principal behaviors and student achievement. One principal action mentioned in the work is the "demonstration of knowledge in curriculum, instruction and assessment." I developed a training called "Leadership 101" that included the following mastery objectives:

1. Possess a general knowledge and understanding of curriculum scope and sequence with a specific focus on alignment.

2. Recognize and be able to discuss issues related to effective instruction and instructional strategies.

3. Perform effective instructional evaluation, including walkthrough observation and teacher evaluation.

4. Analyze various forms of data with a focus on student performance and instructional delivery and the development of a discussion base.

5. Have the ability to give and receive effective feedback that targets improvement and includes affirmation and an evaluative response to promote positive change.

This was a significant shift in thinking and behavior for most of our administrative staff. We met on a regular basis for full days of learning and discussion, and administrators attended training with their teachers regarding curriculum, instruction, and data review. The discussions were rich as they learned right along with the teachers. Administrators learned the skills needed to support the efforts of instructional change while learning to devote more energy and time to teaching and learning.

Over the course of about a year and a half, we were able to refocus curriculum, instruction, and assessment along with the expectations of performance for teachers, students, and administrators. We completed the development of major support materials and text adoptions in just about every grade and content area. Our first real result in student performance appeared in August 2010, when our scores in communication arts and mathematics saw a significant increase. We firmly believe that this improvement was caused by aligning our curricula and instruction to the state standards. Figure 3.1 is an example of the achievement we experienced as a result of this basic work. In the words of the famous cowboy Will Rogers, we were now moving "roughly west."

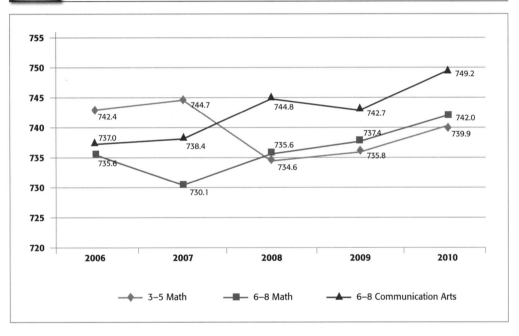

FIGURE 3.1 Increases in Achievement—Math and Communication Arts

As teachers began to experience success in student achievement, they focused more on the work of standardizing practice, which included collaboration in grade levels and content areas, and writing standard units of study and pacing guides. Our high school American government classes provided a specific example of what standardization and focus on standards-based goals and objectives can accomplish (Figure 3.2).

FIGURE
3.2 **Increases in Achievement—American Government**

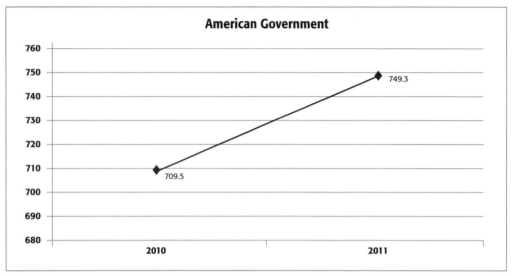

After another year in the process of standardizing our work, we were surprised when our scores were returned in August 2011. They stayed flat or went down slightly in almost all academic areas. We immediately reviewed our data and processes to find reasons for our lack of overall improvement. Our only conclusion was that we needed to focus more on actual instructional planning, delivery, strategies, and techniques to strengthen the curriculum we knew was aligned with the standards. Changes in curriculum also call for changes in instruction. As the associate superintendent, I had a focused goal in mind and I knew that we were headed in the right direction. It was my job to convince the school community that we should not be deterred from our goal but instead perfect it with more focused teaching. We were persistent and did not waiver from our comprehensive plan of specific professional development and curriculum review and revision.

To support teachers in instructional planning and delivery, in the fall of 2011 we began a series on "Champion Teaching" based on the book *Teach Like a Champion* (2010) by Doug Lemov. Teachers went through a semester-long series of classes and building group meetings focused on specific teaching techniques to increase rigor and the quality of instructional delivery. Over half of the teaching staff (480 teachers) took advantage of this learning, were paid for their attendance, and earned three full graduate units of credit offered by two local universities. The work became the topic of discussions in grade-level and content planning meetings and even in the teachers' lounge. This class turned out to be one of the most popular offerings in the district, with most attendees recommending that the work continue with a "Champion Teaching Two" class for 2012. We followed up with a specific walkthrough observation process that assisted administrators in identifying the techniques that were proved to increase rigor and student achievement. These observations prompted discussions between administrators and teachers that were relevant to what was important to the teachers. In some schools, this opened the door for organized efforts by teachers to begin professional learning communities.

With full implementation of the Common Core State Standards adopted by Missouri slated to begin in 2014, we knew that we would have to repeat the entire standardization and curriculum design process again within the next two school years, while still maintaining our current curriculum that was tied to state standards and accountability testing. It was clear that we needed more direct assistance in curriculum development beyond our own studies and reading. This would be a large undertaking and would require the availability and work of many classroom teachers to follow the process to its logical conclusion.

Rigorous Curriculum Design: The Next Phase

We began our official partnership with The Leadership and Learning Center in August 2011. Establishing effective leadership practices was essential to our work, so we started with studies in leadership with our facilitator, Dr. Connie Kamm. We then transitioned into overview and planning for curriculum design to facilitate our work for the future Common Core State Standards coming our way in 2014. We began this work in earnest in December 2011. We also sent a team of district trainers to Data Teams training provided by The Center to complement our work in Rigorous Curriculum Design across the district. Data Teams would be the venue in which we would develop our skills in collaboration, teamwork, and use of data. With the strong background provided by The Center, and the beginning of Data Teams to support the work, the instructional leadership team developed a plan to address our efforts specific to Raytown schools. We have experienced great success as we have worked through the plan for our work and have learned valuable lessons as well. The following is a synopsis of our most recent work.

February 2012: Committees were formed that consisted of a principal facilitator, a cofacilitator, and three teachers for the purpose of reviewing a set of the Common Core State Standards. Groups represented elementary grades K–2, 3–5, 6–8, and 9–12 for both English language arts (ELA) and mathematics. Implementing the first foundational step in the RCD process, each group developed and agreed upon a set of prioritized standards to help our instructional staff focus on the most important skills required of our students. This process provided opportunities for very deep conversation and passionate discussions regarding what students need to know and be able to do. This was a perfect example of why this process is so very valuable for teachers in that it focused discussions on the core beliefs teachers hold regarding teaching and learning.

March 2012: All groups met and completed a gallery walk activity to review the prioritized standards, ensuring vertical alignment from grade to grade and course to course. These prioritized standards represented what students are to know (content) and be able to do (skills) by the end of each academic school year so they are prepared to enter the *next* level of learning. This exercise was so much more useful than just articulated discussions, because teachers had a visual progression on the walls that moved from grade to grade within each content area.

April and May 2012: Committees took the final "Prioritized Standards" back to every building to share with all teaching staff. Facilitators and cofacilitators were asked to gather teacher feedback and submit for final approval what was to be named the *Raytown Common Core Prioritized Standards*. Feedback was reviewed and adjustments were made as needed for clarification. This exercise was very powerful. Teacher facilitators were able to explain the process in their own words, which made the work they had done more accessible to their thoughts and suggestions for the work. The following comments and questions are samples of the feedback that we received.

- "The Rigorous Curriculum Design process so far has allowed for standards that are manageable and not so overwhelming in scope. This focuses the work and our discussions."

- "I appreciate how the teachers are the ones creating this curriculum and how district leaders see the importance of our owning the work. This process has allowed me to take ownership of not only the process, but also the product. I am appreciated for my knowledge and skills."

- "How and when do we work with and/or remediate those who do not have the basic skills for these standards?"

- "This is very overwhelming to me in many ways but also empowering in many others. It makes me think about my profession and my place within it."

- "How will the move happen from our current curriculum to the new one so that students do not lose instruction on specific standards that may be lost in the transition?"

- "The rigor in math is very exciting. I cannot wait to start teaching at this level of critical thinking!"

- "It is raising the expectations of the students and teachers—GREAT!"
- "Reading standards are less about 'skill and drill' and more about true thinking and learning—yeah! Also, the main idea is a concept we think needs to be taught early on, as it is present in the standards."

We believe that our continued work on the design process will allow us to devise a plan for smooth transition. Clearly, teachers have taken ownership in the work and are excited to see it through to its completion.

June–August 2012: Selected teachers from both K–12 math and English have been working in small groups to assign Priority Standards to units of study for each grade and content area. All teacher teams have made it to step 3 of the RCD unit design process (write the Big Ideas and Essential Questions) of designing curricular units. Some groups have reached steps 4 and 5 (create the unit pre- and post-assessments). The district instructional team met together in early August to review each unit completed. Our goal is to provide feedback to each team so they can feel assured they are completing a quality product and are following the Rigorous Curriculum Design steps with fidelity. A scoring guide was developed to assist in providing consistent feedback to all groups. This process has moved slower than expected. However, since we began this process early enough, we have the time to review and revise the instructional units to ensure top quality.

September 2012 and beyond: We plan to continue the process of designing curricular units as we work with The Leadership and Learning Center. We should be ready to pilot units in the spring of 2013. The plan is that each pilot unit will be developed through all 12 steps of the design process and then by February and March 2013 we can release the units to teachers to implement for four to six weeks, depending on the unit length. Our professional learning for teachers will focus on a common vocabulary for this work, increased quality and rigor in instructional planning and delivery, and data review that will promote deep conversation and effective change. We will continue our work in professional learning communities as well because of the clear and powerful link between Rigorous Curriculum Design and a cohesive and collaborative staff, willing to work together for positive results.

Rich conversations between and among teachers are key to their understanding and growth in the process of curriculum development. The process of Rigorous Curriculum Design provides a logical progression that teachers can follow without confusion, making it easy for the teachers to focus conversation where it belongs: on the student.

We have also learned that we must "go slow to go fast." Teachers need time to process information, especially when the expectations of the Common Core are significantly higher than the current state expectations. If the work is hurried, the strength of the work may be compromised and time and energy may be wasted when the process has to be repeated due to the lack of a quality product.

Another realization involves the importance of a district glossary. In order to be on the same page across the district, we must all be speaking the same language in curriculum as well as all other areas that support this work. Common language promotes a common vision and direction and a glossary is an effective way to support this process.

It is a delicate balancing act to remain focused on the current curriculum that is tied to state accountability testing while rewriting the curriculum to match the rigorous Common Core standards. We will need to provide opportunities for teachers to make connections between current and past work in order to successfully bridge to the new system. The goal is to make significant learning progress in all grades. We must be ready for teachers, administrators, and students to build new and improved skills.

Celebrations

Persistence and focus on research and data-proven processes and direction does pay off. In early August 2012, we received our state accountability test scores and we saw progress and results that were the highest the district has experienced since 2007. In some cases, we made more than nine points progress, which is three times more than what the state expects to demonstrate academic progress—a rare accomplishment. This performance was experienced district-wide in just about every grade level and content area. Our community is energized with a sense of pride, making all the change that we have been through together during the last four years definitely worth every moment. We want to keep the momentum going by ensuring that:

- Our district and school communities stay committed to the work;
- We set the bar of expectation high and attainable for everyone involved;
- Achievement growth is sustained by creating an accountability plan that allows for shared responsibility in the educational process.

I am proud to work for a school district with a superintendent, chief financial officer, and board of education that support the work by allowing the educators of the district the freedom to respond to the data and create new practices by funding our efforts to the highest level possible in these difficult budget times. I continue to be amazed at what can be accomplished by a group of professionals focused on a common goal.

It is a shared feeling among district educators that the Common Core State Standards combined with Rigorous Curriculum Design will allow us to create and maintain a curriculum process and product that will stand the test of the rigorous performance assessments coming in the next two years. It is inspiring to watch what a dedicated teacher can do when given a strong curriculum, practiced techniques, and the freedom and power to innovate. Onward!

Getting Started on Your Journey

As you reflect on the Raytown Quality Schools experience, think about how their story applies to you in your current setting, and then answer the following questions:

1. *The first obvious conclusion was that curriculum was not standardized, so actual instruction and specific student expectation was difficult to address as a district, making what data we did have sporadic, unclear, and less useful. Overall, instruction seemed to lack focus on specific learning objectives tied to the state grade and course-level expectations. Informal survey results of staff indicated that many teachers had not reviewed the state standards and no real curriculum was available to them. Classroom visits revealed that there was little common planning of material and lessons. Assessments were, for the most part, teacher-specific and did not match other assessments given by teachers in the same grade or subject.*

   At some point in our educational journeys, we can all relate to at least one of the areas of concern the author mentions in the quote above. Which area of teaching and assessment has been most problematic to you and the other educators in your setting? What steps have you taken to "right the ship"? Explain.

2. In order to make the changes that were necessary in Raytown regarding curriculum design, instruction, and assessment, many out-of-the-box solutions and approaches were found, created, adopted, and implemented. List as many of these as you can recall from the chapter, and highlight the one that stands out to you the most. Then indicate why this particular action resonates with you.

CHAPTER FOUR

McMinnville School District, McMinnville, Oregon

"When we finished the [Rigorous Curriculum Design] overview, the question was simply, 'Do you, as teachers, want this kind of curriculum?' 'Can you see the benefits for yourselves and students?' The answer was an overwhelming 'YES!' In fact, one fifth-grade teacher jumped out of her seat, threw her arms in the air, and said, 'Let's get started!'"

KYRA DONOVAN

"I think the model is a great way to help teachers reach more standards across different subject areas. I like how the performance tasks start at a low Bloom's level and end at a higher level. I struggle with helping my students reach the 'application' level and I think this model will help me get them there."

McMINNVILLE TEACHER

RCD District: McMinnville Public Schools

Location: McMinnville, Oregon (Urban)

Population: 6,473 students

Author: Kyra Donovan, Director of Elementary and Federal Programs

The district demographics of McMinnville Public Schools in Oregon are as follows:

- 6,473 student enrollment;
- 60 percent economically disadvantaged (free/reduced lunch);
- 15 percent limited English proficient;
- 25 percent of students come from homes in which Spanish is the primary language spoken;
- 12 percent students with disabilities;
- 76 percent first-generation (parent without a college degree);
- 65 percent white;
- 31 percent Hispanic;
- 4 percent other ethnicities;
- $40,804 median household income ($7,521 below state average);
- $21,314 per capita average income (among the lowest in the state);
- 17 percent of MSD students live below 130 percent to 185 percent of poverty level;
- 6 elementary schools, 2 middle schools, 1 comprehensive high school.

McMinnville School District Curriculum before RCD

In the past, our district, like many others across the nation, engaged teachers in curriculum mapping based on state standards, curriculum pacing calendars, and curriculum adoptions in kindergarten through high school. We focused on the materials used to teach the content required by our state, and matched those materials to the standards. When asked if we taught to the standards, the answer was, "Well yes, we've been a standards-based education system for a long time."

Then we began asking ourselves:

- "Are we really teaching to the standards?"
- "How do we know?"
- "Do we assess students on the standards, or on the curriculum we've adopted?"
- "How do we know students are truly meeting the standards *before* state assessments take place?"

Common Formative Assessments and Data Teams

In August 2008, our superintendent, Dr. Maryalice Russell, scheduled a two-day Common Formative Assessment (CFA) seminar with facilitators from The Leadership and Learning Center. Laura Besser and Larry Ainsworth presented to both administrators and teacher leaders from all schools. It was our first encounter with the CFA process. I must say we were overwhelmed with all the information and struggled with how we would really be able to develop and implement CFAs in our schools. Again the questions came:

- "Who will write them?"
- "How will we provide the time necessary to develop the CFAs?"
- "What will be the system across the district for *implementation* of the CFAs?"

That same year, we certified some of our administrators in the Data Teams process. We understood that to truly make a difference for student achievement, we needed Data Teams as well as CFAs. And so our journey began . . .

In the fall of 2009 our district implemented a Data Teams system for elementary schools. (Middle school math teachers met as Data Teams as well.) We scheduled monthly district grade-level meetings. Each grade level was facilitated by an elementary principal, and by the director of curriculum and instruction. We targeted math and began with curriculum assessments we felt met the standards. All teachers gave the assessments, gathered their data, and worked in small groups to complete the Data Teams template. Teachers engaged in collaborative discussions about instructional strategies that worked well for students and resources used to meet needs. The conversations were strong and teachers were supportive of each other. What we discovered that year was that a monthly meeting for Data Teams didn't meet the needs of our diverse learners. Some teachers were not ready to give the assessment at the same time as others because they were spending more time reteaching concepts, or moving quicker because students were ready to move on.

Also, during the 2009/10 school year, a group of elementary and middle school math teachers began developing math CFAs. Our goal was to have at least three for each grade level ready to implement the following school year.

In the fall of 2010, we decided to give each elementary and middle school six half-day releases so the grade levels could meet as Data Teams. We felt this was more flexible and created a system for Data Teams that fit teachers' and students' needs better than our monthly meetings the previous year. We had many of the mathematics CFAs developed, but not all. We provided additional time for teachers to continue development. In October, we scheduled another Common Formative Assessments seminar with The Center. Two consultants came, one for math and one for writing. We completed more math CFAs and began developing writing CFAs as well. We were well on our way to implementation.

During that year, it became apparent that more communication was needed with all teachers about the purpose of common formative assessments. The Director of Elementary Programs then visited each school during a staff meeting and explained how CFAs are developed, and that these assessments were completely based on *standards*, not on an adopted curriculum. Our purpose was to assess student knowledge of the standards, not the curriculum, and then use that student data to focus and adjust instruction to meet the various needs of students. After those conversations, our implementation was deeper and much better understood by teachers. The benefits of CFAs became clear to teachers—not only for themselves but also for their students. As teachers administered the CFAs, they submitted any revisions they felt were needed. A team of teachers met during the fall of the following year and made the revisions necessary. As a result, we knew our CFAs had become even stronger.

Our math student achievement results on the Oregon Assessment of Knowledge and Skills (OAKS) that spring were above state average in grades 3–8.

 FIGURE 4.1 Math Student Achievement Results

Grade Level	2010/11 OAKS Math—Points Above State Average
3	9 points One school—31 points
4	11 points Two schools—23 points
5	15 points Two schools—24 points
6	9 points
7	10 points
8	13 points

Rigorous Curriculum Design

Three years after our first experience with common formative assessments and Data Teams (we also had a group of teachers and administrators certified in Power Strategies for Effective Teaching), we were seeing improvement in student achievement, especially math. Yet the CFAs, Power Strategies, and Data Teams still felt a little disjointed. We had curriculum maps with CFAs plugged in where we felt they fit best. We had teachers implementing research-based instructional practices (selected during their Data Team work), but it wasn't quite the "whole" picture. We needed to take the next step.

Larry Ainsworth came to Oregon and presented Rigorous Curriculum Design at a statewide conference in August 2011. During that presentation, the "big picture" became so clear. The RCD model put all the pieces together. We scheduled Larry to come to our district in October. We decided to start unit planning with teachers in fifth, seventh, and eighth grades and with high school language arts teachers. After Larry presented the RCD one-day overview to them, I simply asked the teachers this two-part question: "Do you, as teachers, want this kind of curriculum? Can you see the benefits for yourselves and students?" The answer was an overwhelming "YES!" In fact, one fifth-grade teacher jumped out of her seat, threw her arms in the air and said, "Let's get started!"

The fifth-grade teachers decided they would target science (state-assessed content for Oregon's fifth-grade students). We knew the five foundational RCD steps; Larry had taught us those. However, being new to RCD, we didn't really see the benefit of assigning *all* the standards (content-area state standards and CCSS literacy standards) to units of study and then developing a pacing calendar (RCD foundation steps 3 and 4). We thought we'd jump right into unit development and just follow the RCD unit development template.

Fifth-grade teachers divided into RCD unit teams of two or three teachers each. We selected science standards for each unit and began "unwrapping" them. We filled in the graphic organizer and assigned Bloom's taxonomy levels to the verbs (representing skills students were to be able to do). All was going well until we came to the development of authentic performance tasks. Because this step was very new for us, we decided to wait until Larry came back in February before continuing on.

In January, we shared the Rigorous Curriculum Design one-day overview with fourth-grade teachers and high school science, social studies, and language arts teachers. During that overview we realized we could not continue unit development without doing *all* the foundational steps.

We planned to have Larry come back in February and conduct two additional days of professional development for each grade level and content area to name the units of study, assign the standards (state content standards and CCSS) to the units, and to develop yearlong pacing calendars. After completing that training, *then* we would start unit development. It took a full day to complete the naming of the units, assigning of the standards, and developing of the pacing calendars. We actually had to completely start over with our original fifth-grade science units, because after completing the foundational steps we came to a big "aha": we decided we needed to keep the Common Core ELA standards as our Priority Standards and use the state content standards as the *supporting standards.* This resulted in the creation of *integrated* ELA-science and ELA-social studies units, as well as math units based on the CCSS for elementary grades.

The elementary approach was reversed for the high school content areas. The *content standards* were (correctly) assigned as the Priority Standards and the grades 6–12 CCSS literacy standards as the supporting standards. We wanted to be sure our units focused on the content standards, *as well as* the literacy standards. We scheduled another day to continue unit development with the fourth-, fifth-, seventh-, and eighth-grade teachers, plus language arts at the high school. Because these teachers made up our first district group of curriculum design teams, we referred to them collectively as "RCD Cohort 1."

While this first RCD cohort continued developing their units, we introduced the one-day RCD overview to the third-grade, middle school math, and high school math teachers; these design groups became RCD Cohort 2. They, too, were excited to get started. We followed the same sequence of steps as we had with the first cohort: two days of naming units, assigning Priority Standards and supporting standards to them, developing the pacing calendars, and beginning the actual unit development. But it was now May, and we wondered how we could keep such positive momentum going since it just wasn't possible to schedule additional release days for teachers to work on RCD units before the end of the school year. Yet we needed more time to develop units.

June 18 was the last day for teachers, so we scheduled June 19 and 20, July 16–20, and August 20–22 as Rigorous Curriculum Design "production days." Teachers were paid the curriculum rate for their time to continue developing units of study throughout the summer. We sent an e-mail to all licensed staff members inviting any and all who wanted to be part of the project. If any teachers had not been through the one-day overview but wanted to be a part of the work, we provided them with the RCD overview and then got them started on unit development. Teacher teams formed in grades 3, 4, 5, and 7; eighth-grade language arts, science, and social studies; and high school language arts, social studies, science, and math (algebra I).

During our summer RCD production days, we had 50–60 teachers engaged in unit development spanning third grade through high school! Since the summer work, we've continued to receive e-mails from teachers who have not yet attended the RCD overview indicating that they also want to learn about it and to be involved.

While teachers were engaged in summer unit development, our state test scores for 2011/12 were posted. Again McMinnville School District showed significant gains in student achievement. Math scores continued to go up across our district. As we "rolled out" RCD, we continued implementing our math CFAs, Data Teams, and power strategies. The results shown in the following chart speak for themselves.

FIGURE 4.2 **Math Student Achievement Results**

Grade Level	2010/11 OAKS Math— Points Above State Average	2011/12 OAKS Math— Points Above State Average
3	9 points One school—31 points	20 points Four schools—26+ points
4	11 points Two schools—23 points	17 points
5	15 points Two schools—24 points	19 points
6	9 points	17 points One school—30 points
7	10 points	8 points
8	13 points	12 points

RCD Production Week

RCD production days held during the summer for Cohorts 1 and 2 were extremely successful. We all met in the same building—a small conference center with five rooms. It worked very well to have everyone in the same space. It would have been very difficult to facilitate and answer questions for each group if we had not all been together. Even with the close proximity, at times it was difficult to get to everyone. We learned that having each grade level together supported collaborative conversation regarding the unit assessments, the Common Core State Standards, and performance tasks with matching scoring guides. Teachers asked each other to check their work and understanding of the units and standards. It was imperative in this early stage of RCD production to have everyone in the same facility.

Teachers also had *cross-grade-level* discussions about their units, developing a vertical alignment as well as a horizontal alignment between each grade and content area. Each grade or content-area group subdivided into smaller groups of two to three teachers. These smaller groups each began developing an RCD unit using the RCD templates: the unit planning organizer, unit assessment planner, and the performance tasks planner. Toward the end of the week, each group pulled its entire team of teachers together to review the completed units. They went through each RCD planner for every unit completed. This proved to be very helpful. Teachers were able to focus on the clarity of the units (they were very knowledgeable about the units they wrote, but not as clear on units they didn't write, especially the performance tasks and scoring guides).

As we reviewed the units, we asked ourselves, "Will teachers who are not here with us understand how to implement this unit?" As a result, we revised some of the units, yet still consider them as "works in progress" until we implement the units with students. During classroom implementation this year, design teams will revise the units as they are implemented. For the elementary level, we've already scheduled district-wide grade-level meetings at the end of each quarter in order to edit and/or revise RCD units that have been taught. We will also be scheduling revision meetings for our two middle schools and the high school.

RCD Next Steps

Throughout the 2011/12 school year, our district had a total of 128 teachers in grades 3–12 involved in Rigorous Curriculum Design. By August 22, 2012, we'll complete RCD units for grades 3 through high school. The pacing calendars and completed units will be implemented beginning in the 2012/13 school year. We will not finish *all* of the units, but we'll have enough to begin the implementation phase. During this implementation, we'll have in place an embedded staff development model at each school to continue providing ongoing support and training. This will be important to achieve deep implementation and sustainability.

To continue our goal of writing curricular units for *all* grade levels, we plan to soon begin RCD Cohort 3 with kindergarten, first, and second grades. We'll use the same organizational structure we developed with our first two cohorts.

During the 2012/13 school year, we've planned RCD production days for each grade level and content area. Our vision is to develop a rigorous, standards-based curriculum district-wide that is focused more on "how" we teach, not just on "what" we teach. We are confident that the RCD model will support our teachers and students in meeting the demands of the Common Core State Standards and in better preparing our students for success on the Smarter Balanced Assessment Consortium tests that will be first administered to our students in 2014/15.

What McMinnville Teachers and Administrators Are Saying about RCD

- "I really like the 'backwards design' of the RCD model and think it really falls in line with Power Strategies for Effective Teaching, CFAs, and what we are doing as a school."

- "This model makes clear precisely how our team should be working together for the benefit of all kids."

- "I like the thoroughness of the RCD model and how it really focuses on the standards."

- "I like this model for curriculum design. I believe it will make my life as a teacher easier by mapping out exactly what I need to do to effectively teach and assess my students, as well as giving me better ideas of what my students already know."

> *"RCD will provide a cohesive process throughout McMinnville School District. It will help our instruction be more focused and ensure that our students will have similar content experiences regardless of who is their teacher."*

- "Rigorous Curriculum Design is a great way to remind us to continually go back to the Common Core and make sure we are aligning all of our instruction to the standards."

- "RCD is a perfect fit; I'm excited to see it used K–12."

- "[RCD] honors teachers' individuality while bringing us all together as a district."

- "I think the model is a great way to help teachers connect more standards across different subject areas. I like how the performance tasks start at a lower Bloom's level and end at a higher level. I struggle with helping my students reach the 'application' level and I think this model will help me get them there."

> *"I think this model is not too far from where we currently are. It is exciting to pull all the pieces we've been doing (CFAs, Data Teams, Power Strategies for Effective Teaching) together. It will make every moment in my classroom count!"*

- "This model brings together Data Teams, research-based strategies, CFAs, and the CCSS in a way that makes sense and shows how each component is related to the others."

- "[The RCD framework] will allow for a more comprehensive and consistent implementation of the CCSS, and give teachers a systematic method to succeed."

Sean Burke, McMinnville High School Vice Principal of Curriculum and Instruction who has facilitated the development of the RCD units completed by his various high school department teachers, writes: "The RCD process gave our teachers at the high school a chance to bring all of the components of effective teaching together and it made them consider other support structures for our special education and ELL students. On another level, it provided our staff with the realization that the CFAs were not just another step in teaching. Instead, they really did provide us with the feedback we needed in order to adjust our instruction and to provide specific structures for students who needed them. As a result, our teachers, who in the beginning felt we already had CFAs in place, now see that we had 'something on paper' but it was not providing the student data they needed. This was a major step for our high school staff to take. It's one thing to go through the motions of curriculum unit design. But when a teacher realizes that results for students aren't good enough and begins to look inward while collaboratively discussing instruction with colleagues, it's something more. Teachers are now trying to decide whether it is the use of a specific strategy, the design of the assessment, or something else that results in students not learning the intended knowledge and skills."

Our RCD Vision

The McMinnville School District Rigorous Curriculum Design vision is a system of both vertical and horizontal alignment of standards, based on common Essential Questions and Big Ideas, assessments, and authentic performance tasks. This vision will determine our K–12 curriculum for all content areas. We've had great success with CFAs, Data Teams, and Power Strategies for Effective Teaching. Rigorous Curriculum Design will strengthen instruction, assessment, and collaboration across our district, and with that we are confident that we will attain outstanding student achievement at all levels. To quote our superintendent, Dr. Russell, it's always about: "Student Achievement! Student Achievement! Student Achievement."

Getting Started on Your Journey

As you reflect on the McMinnville Public Schools account, think about how their story applies to you in your current setting, and then answer the following questions:

1. *When asked if we taught to the standards, the answer was, "Well yes, we've been a standards-based education system for a long time."*

   Then we began asking ourselves:
   - *"Are we really teaching to the standards?"*
   - *"How do we know?"*
   - *"Do we assess students on the standards, or the curriculum we've adopted?"*
   - *"How do we know students are truly meeting the standards before state assessments take place?*

   Thinking about standards implementation in your setting, what are your answers to each of the questions above that McMinnville educators asked in order to ascertain where the district truly was with regard to standards and assessment?

2. *That same year, we certified some of our administrators in Data Teams. We understood that to truly make a difference in student achievement, we needed Data Teams as well as CFAs.*

   What processes or strategies does your school/district use when it comes to ongoing use of data to drive decision making? How does this approach align with curricular design at your site? Explain.

3. *Our purpose was to assess student knowledge on the standards, not the curriculum, and then use that student data to focus and adjust instruction to meet the various needs of students.*

   This comment from the chapter represents a paradigm shift in curricular and instructional thought and purpose for McMinnville. Describe a recent change in thinking your school or district has experienced lately. What actions did you take as a result? What actions were altered?

CHAPTER FIVE

West Hartford Public Schools, West Hartford, Connecticut

"West Hartford is a high-performing school district with the vision that high expectations for all learners, rigorous and relevant curriculum, and dynamic teaching inspire a passion for learning and help all students realize their potential. We have always worked in the best interest of our students, but consistency and coherence across the curriculum were not well defined. As a result, the text became the curriculum and the level of rigor and expectations varied across the schools. What we have done this year in adopting the Rigorous Curriculum Design model, prioritizing the Common Core State Standards, and raising rigor and relevance through our units will define our future."

"It was extremely rewarding to see our first units take shape and reflect on how far we had come over a four-month span of time. One participant aptly summed up the experience when stating that the most beneficial part of this process was 'being able to discuss curriculum with colleagues K–12; seeing the vertical alignment we never have time to see; having time to have meaningful discussions on curriculum.'"

SALLY ALUBICKI

RCD District: West Hartford Public Schools

Location: West Hartford, Connecticut
(Suburban)

Population: 10,000 students

Author: Sally Alubicki, Ed.D., Director of
Teaching and Assessment

The town of West Hartford, located in central Connecticut, is home to approximately 60,000 residents. We have 10,000 students attending 16 schools, with the total school population more than 37 percent minority. Approximately 19 percent of this district's students come from homes where English is not the primary language, and there are 65 different languages represented in the school system. English for speakers of other languages (ESOL) is provided in all schools, and bilingual programs are required in five schools. Over the past six years, full-day prekindergarten programs have been established in five elementary schools, with tuition based on a sliding scale.

West Hartford is a study in contrasts. It is one of the few communities whose percentage of minority students and percentage of students eligible for free or reduced lunch are both within 15 percentage points of the state average. Five of our schools qualify for Title I services. In 2010, West Hartford was named one of the nation's "10 Great Cities for Raising Families" by *Kiplinger's Personal Finance* magazine. That same year, Kiplinger's also ranked West Hartford number nine on its "10 Best Cities for the Next Decade." While we continue to focus on reducing the achievement gap in our schools, the diversity and merging of cultures is what makes this such an exciting and rewarding school system in which to work.

Impetus for Change

Ten years ago, the Curriculum Professional Development Council (CPDC) was established to provide district-wide coordination of curriculum and implementation. The CPDC includes school administrators, central office staff, teachers, department supervisors, and curriculum specialists, and is facilitated by the assistant superintendent for instruction and curriculum. All curricular areas are evaluated on a five-year cycle, and a timeline is in place for department evaluation, presentation to the CPDC, and subsequent implementation of changes as a result of the evaluation. The cycle of review is represented in Figure 5.1.

Since this process was new to West Hartford, the first time a curriculum came up for review, the department supervisors and curriculum specialists basically provided a status report of the curriculum, as well as short- and long-term goals. In the next review (five years later) the process was repeated with reference made to goals that had been accomplished and plans for future change. Since the curriculum was based on state standards, and those standards reflected our state assessments, the Connecticut Mastery Test and Connecticut Academic Performance Test (CMT and CAPT), we basically had a test-driven curriculum.

A very important change was made to this process when Dr. Eileen Howley became Assistant Superintendent for Instruction and Curriculum in 2009. While the existing

FIGURE 5.1 Long-Range Curriculum/Program Planning Calendar

Curriculum Area	2006 2007	2007 2008	2008 2009	2009 2010	2010 2011	2011 2012	2012 2013	2013 2014
Theatre 9–12	Eval	Plan	Imp 1	Imp 2	Imp 3	Eval	Plan	Imp 1
Library/Media K–12	Imp 3	Eval	Plan	Imp 1	Imp 2	Imp 3	Eval	Plan
Mathematics K–12	Imp 3	Eval	Plan	Imp 1	Imp 2	Imp 3	Eval	Plan
REACH & AIMS	Imp 3	Eval	Plan	Imp 1	Imp 2	Imp 3	Eval	Plan
ESOL K–12	Imp 2	Imp 3	Eval	Plan	Imp 1	Imp 2	Imp 3	Eval
Health Education/Substance Abuse K–12	Imp 2	Imp 3	Eval	Plan	Imp 1	Imp 2	Imp 3	Eval
Music K–12	Imp 2	Imp 3	Eval	Plan	Imp 1	Imp 2	Imp 3	Eval
Physical Education K–12	Imp 2	Imp 3	Eval	Plan	Imp 1	Imp 2	Imp 3	Eval
World Language K–12	Imp 2	Imp 3	Eval	Plan	Imp 1	Imp 2	Imp 3	Eval
Gifted Education	Imp 1	Imp 2	Imp 3	Eval	Plan	Imp 1	Imp 2	Imp 3
Science K–12	Imp 1	Imp 2	Imp 3	Eval	Plan	Imp 1	Imp 2	Imp 3
Social Studies K–12	Imp 1	Imp 2	Imp 3	Eval	Plan	Imp 1	Imp 2	Imp 3
Art K–12	Plan	Imp 1	Imp 2	Imp 3	Eval	Plan	Imp 1	Imp 2
Language Arts/English K–12	Plan	Imp 1	Imp 2	Imp 3	Eval	Plan	Imp 1	Imp 2
School Counseling	Plan	Imp 1	Imp 2	Imp 3	Eval	Plan	Imp 1	Imp 2
Technology Education 6–12 (includes Business Education 9–12, School to Career, and Family and Consumer Science 9–12)	Plan	Imp 1	Imp 2	Imp 3	Eval	Plan	Imp 1	Imp 2

Eval (Evaluation) Year: Begins no later than second half of year commencing in January. Instructions for evaluation process are described in the Five Year Plan for Curriculum Review document available in the Office of Curriculum and Instruction and each school in our district.

Plan Year: 1. CPDC October/November presentation of evaluation.
2. Budget priorities identified.

Imp (Implementation Year): Implementation of changes as a result of evaluation/planning.

model for reviewing curriculum was an excellent start, she raised the rigor of the process by including curriculum vertical teams, intensifying the need for analysis of data, establishing ad hoc work groups to address the issues, challenges, and/or needs that were identified by the vertical team, and providing a rubric for rating various areas of the curriculum. What became obvious through this process was that there was no agreed-upon model for curriculum design across content areas. Curriculum was based on ever-changing state standards, not always taught using the resources available but rather based on what teachers "like to teach." So, we asked ourselves what should be the agreed-upon design for curriculum that would provide coherence across the disciplines and maintain rigorous standards. This became our first impetus for change.

Our second rationale for change came in July 2010 when the Connecticut State Board of Education adopted the Common Core State Standards (CCSS) for English language arts and mathematics. The Connecticut standards on which we had built our curriculum were no longer in place, and it became quickly evident that the CCSS were much more rigorous than those we had been using. Our state curriculum leaders developed crosswalk documents to show the correlation between Common Core State Standards and Connecticut standards. While we would continue teaching many of the same skills and strategies, it was obvious that the college- and career-readiness anchor standards for English language arts provided in the CCSS made it necessary for us to "ramp up" our curriculum—especially if we expected students to exhibit the capacities of literate individuals who are college- and career-ready in reading, writing, speaking, listening, and language.

As with many other districts in Connecticut, we prepared our students to meet the demands of the state tests. Our approach was quite formulaic and involved a lot of test prep. With the adoption of the Common Core State Standards, Connecticut was identified as one of the governing states for the Smarter Balanced Assessment Consortium (SBAC), one of two multistate consortia that were building systems of assessment based on the CCSS. SBAC would develop an assessment system to measure higher-order thinking skills and inform progress and acquisition of readiness for multiple work domains. It was obvious that an assessment that would measure problem solving, analysis, synthesis, and critical thinking was not a test we could "teach to." We needed curricula that included the rigor and relevance to truly help our students achieve high standards. Coincidentally, this concept already existed in the district mission: "to inspire and prepare all students to realize their potential and enhance our global community."

At this point, we knew we needed a consistent curriculum design model and we realized our existing curriculum did not embody the rigor of the Common Core State

Standards nor would it prepare our students to meet with success on the SBAC assessments.

After providing crosswalk documents, state-level curriculum design teams prioritized the CCSS and developed a set of foundational documents using Larry Ainsworth's Rigorous Curriculum Design (RCD) model. While the intention was not to develop a state curriculum for districts, it was a way to help us develop our own curriculum that embodied the Common Core. We purchased Larry's book, *Rigorous Curriculum Design: How to Create Curricular Units of Study that Align Standards, Instruction, and Assessment* (2010). We attended a summit sponsored by The Leadership and Learning Center in New Haven, Connecticut, in September, 2011. During that summit, Larry shared his 12-step design for curricular units and we quickly saw the potential for using that as our model in West Hartford. It included all of the components we needed to enhance instruction, and would provide a way to bring about the consistency in teaching and learning that we were striving for. The next question was a big one: How would we pull it off?

Implementing the Rigorous Curriculum Design Model

With the approval of Dr. Karen List, Superintendent of Schools, we contracted with The Leadership and Learning Center to have Larry spend nine days in our district working with our administrators and teachers to write units based on his design model. We met with Larry prior to beginning this work to share the culture of our district and our perceived curriculum strengths and weakness. Throughout the upcoming yearlong process, there was a consistent thread: Larry was continually responsive to our needs and both his knowledge of curriculum and positive manner helped us realize we could make a monumental change.

We selected a total of nine dates in January, February, April, and May of 2012 during which our curriculum design team would work with Larry. It was critical that we include teachers, curriculum specialists, and department supervisors in the work. Building principals at the elementary level and department supervisors, along with school administrators at the secondary level, selected teacher participants. We developed criteria for selecting curriculum design team members that included teachers who:

- Had exhibited leadership qualities and could successfully share this work with other colleagues;
- Had exhibited expertise in teaching English language arts and mathematics;

- Had the ability to plan coherent, meaningful lessons for their students during the nine days they would be absent from the classroom;

- Could commit to summer curriculum writing time if needed.

In addition to the above, we needed teachers who were respected by their peers and had a positive attitude about change. We were fortunate to assemble an amazing group of educators who brought energy and thoughtfulness to the work. Prior to beginning this project, we provided each participant with a copy of Larry's book and the Common Core State Standards. We also requested that, throughout this process, the RCD team members report progress back to their buildings and departments. We wanted all of our work to be public and, since we couldn't include every teacher on the writing teams, we wanted all staff members to have a high level of awareness of the process and impending curriculum changes.

Our curriculum team members represented all 16 schools. One of the things special to West Harford Public Schools is the position of curriculum specialist (CS). Each elementary school has a CS who, among other things, is responsible for curriculum implementation. Our elementary team included six curriculum specialists (all of whom had classroom experience) and six classroom teachers. This group was led by Jennifer Parsons, our district elementary reading/language arts curriculum specialist. Facilitated by Paul Vicinus, director of secondary education, and Christine Newman, elementary curriculum specialist for math and science, we were also creating RCD units in elementary and secondary mathematics as part of this curriculum redesign project. But we realized we couldn't expect each elementary teacher to implement new ELA and math units at the same time. Therefore, our ELA teams developed units for kindergarten and grades 2 and 4, while math focused on grades 1, 3, and 5. We'll implement those units during the 2012/13 school year. New units for mathematics and ELA for K–5 will be fully developed and implemented by the end of the 2013/14 school year.

At the secondary level, we had eight teachers representing grades 6–10, and the work was facilitated by English department supervisors Catherine Buchholz and Tom Paleologopoulos. Their goal is to teach new ELA units in grades 6–10 during the 2012/13 school year and develop grade 11 RCD units to be implemented in the fall of 2013.

During our first three-day session with Larry in January 2012, he shared his definition for a unit of study and we discussed important aspects of a unit. We then moved on to the very thought-provoking task of prioritizing the Common Core State Standards. We worked in grade-span content-area groups of K–2, 3–5, 6–8, and 9–12. We immediately decided that we did not want to simply use the prioritized CCSS selections that had been determined by the Connecticut State Department teams; rather, we wanted to decide for ourselves what was in the best interest of students in West Hartford Public Schools. (Interestingly enough, we never did look at the priorities that had been identified by the state department group because we felt confident in the selections that resulted from our own direct experience with the process.) There was one aspect of this task that took some getting used to: we would consider all standards as either priority or supporting, but *all* standards would be assigned to our units. In the past, when we had prioritized state standards, we taught the priorities and simply dropped whatever didn't fit in that category. This combined priority/supporting process that Larry moved us through led to much rich discussion.

In English language arts, we began by prioritizing the standards for the informational text strand in our grade-level bands. When completed, we came together as a K–12 group and shared our priorities along with the rationale for our selections. We wanted to see alignment across the priorities and, if it didn't exist, to determine how/if the supporting standards formed the threads needed to provide curricular coherence. We next followed this same process with the CCSS in the literature strand. We then prioritized the writing standards, followed by the speaking and listening standards. The elementary group decided to prioritize the two K–5 strands of foundational skills and language standards during our summer curriculum work.

Our January session ended by naming units of study and assigning Priority Standards and supporting standards to those units. At this point, we were experiencing some cognitive dissonance, as we had our existing curriculum and core materials in mind while we tried to develop new units that didn't include those resources. But, we had faith that we could move on. Teacher comments on this work were decidedly positive, with the following exemplifying the thoughts of the majority:

> *"The process for prioritizing standards was modeled and conducted in a hands-on way so all participants could see, hear, and understand the K–12 continuum. Larry's guidance and knowledge of what has/hasn't worked for others really helped us stay focused and on track when we were headed toward derailment."*

Our work in February focused on foundation step 4 (prepare grade-specific and course-specific pacing calendars) and step 5 (construct the unit planning organizer) of the Rigorous Curriculum Design model. We had scheduled two days for this work and, while we had some K–12 collaboration, much of our time was spent in our grade-level bands. Larry's flexibility was key, as the elementary and secondary teams had not settled on using the unit template that he provided but instead began drafting a unit planner of their own. As long as we had the core features of the RCD model, we knew we would stay true to the process. We also didn't want to slip in the level of rigor and simply revert back to our previous way of writing curriculum. At the conclusion of our work in February, the elementary team was trying to determine where and how our core anthology would fit into the new units. The middle school teachers were struggling with how they would have enough time in the school year to teach and assess all of the standards for mastery. They decided they would need to develop fewer units or have more time for English language arts instruction.

The enthusiasm of the team members never waned and we charged into our April work with even greater purpose. It was time to "unwrap" the standards, and since we had previous experience "unwrapping" state standards, this was a fairly routine task. What proved to be a meatier task was determining the Big Ideas and Essential Questions. It was at this point that our elementary ELA and mathematics groups met together, because we needed to establish a unified definition for each of those concepts. The strength of each unit rested on clear and coherent Big Ideas with Essential Questions that would lead students to discover the Big Ideas.

During April, Larry also shared valuable information on aspects of the SBAC tests as well as key points to remember in writing assessments. Since most participants were not familiar with assessments that had been released by the Smarter Balanced Assessment Consortium, this created a heightened awareness of the rigor of the standards represented in the SBAC test questions. This was particularly important, as we also entered into a discussion of Bloom's Taxonomy and Webb's Depth of Knowledge (DOK). The SBAC assessments use the rigor of DOK, and we needed to be sure our units reflected the same. Larry shared Karin Hess' cognitive rigor matrices and curricular examples, in which she applies the four levels of DOK to the revised Bloom's Taxonomy. True analysis of DOK will be a focus for the district in the fall of 2012, with professional development for staff on this topic.

May 16 and 17 were our final two days of work with Larry. We were able to develop meaningful "assured learning experiences" (authentic performance tasks) that all students would engage in, and to begin designing pre- and post-assessments for each unit of study. It was extremely rewarding to see our first units take shape and to reflect on how far we had come over a four-month span of time. One participant aptly summed up the experience when stating that the most beneficial part of this process was "being able to discuss curriculum with colleagues K–12; seeing the vertical alignment we never have time to see; having time to have meaningful discussions on curriculum."

Next Steps

While we accomplished a great deal during the nine days of RCD work, we knew we needed additional time to prepare units for teachers to use during the course of the upcoming school year. We also needed to share Unit 1 with teachers before the close of school, since we expected them to implement it upon returning in the fall. Throughout the four months of RCD work, the secondary department supervisors had the opportunity to keep all English teachers abreast of the new units during their department meeting time. That time didn't exist for elementary teachers, but we did have a staff professional development day scheduled for June 21, immediately following the last day for students. While this may not seem like an opportune time, it turned out to be a positive experience for all participants.

Jennifer Parsons, our district curriculum specialist, planned the presentation that would include all kindergarten, grade 2, and grade 4 teachers as well as associated staff (special education, gifted and talented, English for speakers of other languages [ESOL], etc.). She began the morning by likening our RCD work to building a home: the Common Core State Standards were the foundation, the RCD team members were the architects, and the unit planner was our blueprint. Since the majority of teachers had limited familiarity with the CCSS, Jennifer led them through a review of those new standards and then followed with information about the revised Bloom's Taxonomy and Webb's Depth of Knowledge. She concluded with a brief snapshot of what Unit 1 included. Basically, she very effectively pared down our nine days of work with Larry into a one-hour overview. At that point, teachers moved to individual grade-level groups and the curriculum specialists who had been RCD participants led them through a thorough review of the first unit, which they would begin implementing in September. One very powerful aspect of the morning included discussion of the pacing guide for grade 4 (Figure 5.2), which would provide structure for the school year.

In their written reflections at the end of this session, teachers were overwhelmingly positive, offering remarks such as:

- "I'm excited to focus on the Big Ideas and Essential Questions for each unit. I appreciate the balance between teaching the unit and including some of my own creativity."

- "I can tell by looking at the unit planner that my lessons will be more meaningful and purposeful. We'll have clear lessons connected to the new standards."

Just as important as the positive comments were the *questions* posed. These included, among other things, how we would communicate changes to parents, how ESOL and special education staff would support the standards, and when/how we would be able to integrate science and social studies topics into the units. Clearly, we have our work cut out for us as we enter the 2012/13 school year.

FIGURE
5.2 **Pacing Guide**

Sequence of Units—Grade 4				
Unit	**Unit Dates**	**Title**	**Number of Instructional Days + "Buffer"**	**Curriculum CSI Dates**
1	9/4/12 – 10/16/12	Elements of Fiction (Literary story elements, character analysis, finding evidence, point of view, narrative writing, collaborative conversations)	25 + 3	Content: 6/21 & 9/5 Collaboration: 9/19
AIMSweb Benchmark: September 10–14				
2	10/17/12 – 11/16/12	Theme (Theme, summarizing literature, literary structures, multiple presentations of text, narrative writing, sentence structure)	20 + 2	Content: 10/3 Collaboration: 10/24
3	11/19/12 – 12/21/12	Features of Nonfiction (Structure of informational texts, informational text features, informational writing, listening to a speaker)	20 + 3	Content: 11/6 Collaboration: 12/5
4	1/2/13 – 2/11/13	Main Idea (Main idea and key details, supporting evidence, informational writing, short research projects, collaborative conversations)	25 + 3	Content: 1/2 Collaboration: 1/23
AIMSweb Benchmark: January 7–11				
	2/12/13 – 3/15/13	Opportunity to Reteach & Introduce Tests as a Genre + CMT Testing Window	19	2/6 2/27
5	3/18/13 – 5/2/13	Using Informational Text to Support Ideas (Events, procedures, ideas and concepts in informational texts, first hand vs. second hand accounts, connections between multiple informational texts, opinion writing, publishing with technology)	25 + 3	Content: 3/6 Collaboration: 4/10
6	5/3/13 – 6/7/13	Mythology (Compare and contrast themes and patterns of events in traditional literature, figurative language, first vs. third person narration, performance and presentation)	20 + 2	Content: 4/24 Collaboration: 5/29
AIMSweb Benchmark: May 13–17				
Total Instructional Days including "Buffer" Days			**170**	

Continuing the RCD Process

The RCD teams were not finished with unit writing at the close of the 2011/12 school year. Dr. Howley had allocated a substantial amount of summer curriculum writing funds, and our elementary and secondary teams took advantage of four full days to continue writing their units of study. As a result of this summer work, we'll be able to distribute units that will be implemented through December. The elementary team members also committed to an additional nine days of work during the 2012/13 school year to complete the kindergarten, grade 2, and grade 4 units, respond to suggestions for revision, and begin to write units for grades 1, 3, and 5, which will be implemented in 2013/14. The secondary team will continue their work during their department meeting time.

It is one thing to prepare and distribute units of instruction, but successful implementation in the classroom can't take place without continued professional development and collaboration among teachers. We're very fortunate in West Hartford that, for over twenty years, we have had two hours of time for staff development scheduled every week. This curriculum and staff instruction (CSI) time takes place every Wednesday. Students are on an early dismissal schedule and teachers have a structured time that is divided between building initiatives and district expectations.

Figure 5.2: Elementary CSI Plan

Figure 5.2 also depicts, in the far right column, the typical schedule for elementary teachers, with CSI time divided between a discussion around unit structure and collaboration. For example, on June 21, teachers received their first unit and had an opportunity to discuss the *content*. That will continue for two hours on the afternoon of September 5, as teachers will have just begun teaching Unit 1, and we anticipate there will be a need to further clarify components of the lessons in that unit. On September 19, support staff such as ESOL and special education will join the classroom teachers and *collaborate* on various aspects of the unit. They will have an opportunity to share ideas about differentiating instruction based on student need, discuss how support staff can reinforce teaching the standards, and analyze specific student success or needs for additional intervention. Built into all of this *content/collaboration* time will be continued focus on the professional learning needs for teachers that have become evident during this RCD work.

The secondary ELA team also has a plan (Figure 5.3) for their CSI time. They have included additional time for writing units, discussing common language for assessment practices, and incorporating 21st-century skills into their units. Their collaborative team time will be structured around a 6–8 and 9–12, or 6–12, configuration as needed. We believe we have an effective plan in place for writing our new curriculum and implementing it in a way that will positively impact student achievement.

FIGURE
5.3   **Secondary CSI Plan**

Week of 8/27	27-Aug Convocation	28-Aug Building 8:00-11:30 C. Team 11:30-12:30 Dept. 1:30-3:30	29-Aug Bldg – NEASC C. Team 3:30-4:30 First Day of Classes	30-Aug	1-Sep

8/27: The goal of convocation is to welcome new and returning staff, celebrate accomplishments of the past year, and chart the course for the district in the coming year; building and department meetings may follow similar themes at that smaller level.

8/28: The goal of department time on 8/28 is to outline the first semester professional development plan, to review the new and revised secondary assessment calendar, to review CMT/CAPT performance data, and make preparations for the beginning of the school year. **8/28 and 8/29:** The goal of Collaborative Team time on 8/28 and 8/29 is to establish school-based team work protocols.

Week of 9/3	3-Sep Labor Day School Holiday	4-Sep	5-Sep PK–12 Department 6–12 Department	6-Sep Collaborative Team Mtg–CCSS	7-Sep

9/5: Teachers will work in town-wide, grade, or course-level collaborative teams; focus of the training will be in and around the Department Development Plan as well as the roll-out of newly developed curriculum units.

9/6: Collaborative team time in schools will be used for roll-out and development of the first units, including lesson planning, looking at student work, development of assessments and performance tasks, and development of instructional strategies for unit implementation.

Week of 9/10	10-Sep Collaborative Team Mtg–CCSS	11-Sep Faculty Meeting Collaborative Team	12-Sep Building– NEASC	13-Sep Collaborative Team Mtg	14-Sep

9/10 and 9/13: Teachers will work in school-based collaborative teams to align **expectations for grading, homework and other logistical policies.**

9/11: School-based PD on successful practices of collaborative teams.

Week of 9/17	17-Sep School Holiday	18-Sep	19-Sep PK–12 Department 6–12 Department	20-Sep Collaborative Team Mtg–CCSS	21-Sep

9/19: Town-wide department will focus on the **Essential Questions and Big Ideas** of the curriculum units and how to use them in instruction.

9/20: Teachers will work in their school-based teams on Essential Questions and Big Ideas.

Week of 9/24	24-Sep Collaborative Team Mtg–CCSS	25-Sep	26-Sep School Holiday	27-Sep Collaborative Team Mtg–CCSS	28-Sep

9/24 and 9/27: Teachers will work in school-based teams on unit planning and instructional strategies to support CCSS units.

Week of 10/1	1-Oct Collaborative Team Mtg–CCSS	2-Oct	3-Oct PK–12 Department 6–12 Department	4-Oct Collaborative Team Mtg–CCSS	5-Oct

10/1: Teachers will work in school-based teams on daily planning and instructional strategies to support CCSS units.

10/3: Town-wide department will work on a common language for **authentic assessment practices,** including **performance tasks for units.**

10/4: Teachers will work in school-based teams on **unit assessments.**

Week of 10/8	8-Oct School Holiday	9-Oct Faculty Meeting	10-Oct Building–NEASC Collaborative Teams	11-Oct Collaborative Team Mtg–CCSS	12-Oct

10/10: Teachers will work in their school-based teams on unit planning and instructional strategies.

10/11: Teachers will work in their school-based teams on unit assessments and/or performance tasks.

FIGURE
5.3
Secondary CSI Plan *(continued)*

Week of 10/15	15-Oct Collaborative Team Mtg–CCSS	16-Oct	17-Oct PLACE	18-Oct Collaborative Team Mtg–CCSS	19-Oct

10/15: Teachers will work in their school-based teams on unit planning and instructional strategies.
10/18: Teachers will work in their building teams on unit assessments and/or performance tasks.
10/17: Teachers can use PLACE time at their high schools for course-wide conversations across standard and honors levels.

Week of 10/22	22-Oct Collaborative Team Mtg–CCSS	23-Oct	24-Oct PK–12 Department 6–12 Department	25-Oct Collaborative Team Mtg–CCSS	26-Oct

10/22: Teachers will work in school-based teams on unit planning and instructional strategies.
10/24: Town-wide department will work on a common language for **21st-century skills** and how they are incorporated in ELA instruction 6–12.
10/25: Teachers will work in their school-based teams on 21st-century skill implementation.

Week of 10/29	29-Oct Collaborative Team Mtg–CCSS	30-Oct	31-Oct Building–NEASC Collaborative Teams	1-Nov Collaborative Team Mtg–CCSS	2-Nov

All week, collaborative teams will work on **review of units** for the first quarter.

Week of 11/5	5-Nov Collaborative Team Mtg–CCSS	6-Nov Secondary Bullying Workshop	7-Nov Parent Conf Prep	8-Nov Collaborative Team Mtg–CCSS	9-Nov

11/5 and 11/8: Teachers will work in school-based teams on unit assessments and performance tasks.

Week of 11/12	12-Nov Collaborative Team Mtg–CCSS	13-Nov Faculty Meeting Collaborative Teams	14-Nov Parent Conferences	15-Nov Collaborative Team Mtg – CCSS	16-Nov

All week, teachers will work in their teams on unit implementation.

Week of 11/19	19-Nov Collaborative Team Mtg–CCSS	20-Nov	21-Nov No CSI activities	22-Nov School Holiday	23-Nov School Holiday

11/19: Teachers work in school-based teams on unit implementation.

Week of 11/26	26-Nov Collaborative Team Mtg–CCSS	27-Nov	28-Nov Building–NEASC Collaborative Teams	29-Nov Collaborative Team Mtg–CCSS	30-Nov

Teachers will work in school-based teams on development of midterm or midyear exams or performance tasks.

Week of 12/3	3-Dec Collaborative Team Mtg–CCSS	4-Dec	5-Dec PK–12 Department 6–12 Department	6-Dec Collaborative Team Mtg–CCSS	7-Dec

12/5: Town-wide department PD on **Webb's Depth of Knowledge.**

FIGURE
5.3 **Secondary CSI Plan** *(continued)*

Week of 12/10	10-Dec Collaborative Team Mtg—CCSS	11-Dec Faculty Meeting Collaborative Team?	12-Dec CSI Series	13-Dec Collaborative Team Mtg—CCSS	14-Dec

CSI Series: English language arts, social studies, and science teachers meet in the town hall auditorium to establish foundation for cross-disciplinary connections.
Collaborative Team Meetings: School-based team follow-up.

Week of 12/17	17-Dec Collaborative Team Mtg—CCSS	18-Dec	19-Dec CSI Series	20-Dec Collaborative Team Mtg—CCSS	21-Dec

CSI Series: English language arts, social studies, and science teachers meet in the town hall auditorium to establish foundation for cross-disciplinary connections.
Collaborative Team Meetings: School-based team follow-up.

Week of 12/24	24-Dec School Holiday	25-Dec School Holiday	26-Dec School Holiday	27-Dec School Holiday	28-Dec School Holiday

Week of 12/31	31-Dec School Holiday	1-Jan School Holiday	2-Jan Building – NEASC Collaborative Teams	3-Jan Collaborative Team Mtg—CCSS	4-Jan

1/2 and 1/3: Review of units taught so far, and preparation for Semester 2.

Week of 1/7	7-Jan Collaborative Team Mtg—CCSS	8-Jan Faculty Meeting	9-Jan CSI Series	10-Jan Collaborative Team Mtg—CCSS	11-Jan

CSI Series: English language arts, social studies, and science teachers meet in the town hall auditorium to establish foundation for cross-disciplinary connections.
Collaborative Team Meetings: School-based team follow-up.

Week of 1/14	14-Jan Collaborative Team Mtg—CCSS	15-Jan	16-Jan Building—NEASC Collaborative Teams	17-Jan Collaborative Team Mtg—CCSS	18-Jan

1/14, 1/16, and 1/17: Exam prep, academic interventions.

Week of 1/21	21-Jan School Holiday	22-Jan	23-Jan High School Exams	24-Jan Collaborative Team Mtg—CCSS	25-Jan

1/24: Unit planning for Semester 2.

Final Thoughts

West Hartford is a high-performing school district with the vision that "high expectations for all learners, rigorous and relevant curriculum, and dynamic teaching inspire a passion for learning and help all students realize their potential." We have always worked in the best interest of our students, but consistency and coherence across the curriculum were not well defined. As a result, the text became the curriculum and the level of rigor and expectations varied across the schools. What we have done this year in adopting the Rigorous Curriculum Design model, prioritizing the Common Core State Standards, and raising rigor and relevance through our units will define our future.

We had compelling reasons to move to the Rigorous Curriculum Design model. We believe it will enable our teachers to connect curriculum, instruction, and assessment while implementing the Common Core State Standards. While it's too early to tell, we are confident the result will be increased student achievement. However, diving into a project like this is not for the faint of heart, and there are many things that need to be in place in order to have it come to a successful conclusion. Included among them:

- Compelling and accepted reasons for making a change;
- District leadership that is visible and focused on the project;
- Bringing in an external expert to lead the work—internal expertise is essential, but the power of someone who has led this charge across the country brings a new perspective;
- Funding to provide the resources necessary for educators to teach the new units;
- Time for continued professional learning for teachers.

One teacher summed it up quite well: "I have always felt valued as a teacher in West Hartford, but I have not experienced the enthusiasm within myself or from others as when we reviewed our first new unit. The excitement around collaboration built into this will heighten the level of my teaching and what my students will learn. Thank you!"

Getting Started on Your Journey

As you reflect on the account of West Hartford Public Schools' experience, think about how their story applies to you in your current setting, and then answer the following questions:

1. *As with many other districts in Connecticut, we prepared our students to meet the demands of the state tests. It was quite formulaic and involved a lot of test prep.*

   Did you feel this way during the standards 1.0 movement (focus on state-specific standards)? Do you still feel this way today as you are implementing the CCSS? If so, what adult behaviors foster this type of environment? If not, what deliberate practices do you implement to ensure this is not the case? Explain.

2. *We immediately decided that we did not want to simply use the prioritized selections that had been determined by the Connecticut State Department teams; rather, we wanted to decide for ourselves what was in the best interest of students in West Hartford Public Schools. (Interestingly enough, we never did look at the priorities that had been identified by the state department group because we felt confident in the selections that resulted from our own direct experience with the process.) There was one aspect of this task that took some getting used to: we would consider all standards as either priority or supporting, but all standards would be assigned to our units.. In the past when we had prioritized state standards, we taught the priorities and simply dropped whatever didn't fit in that category. This combined priority/supporting process that Larry moved us through led to much rich discussion.*

   The notion of prioritizing the Common Core State Standards has generated lively discussions, thoughts, and opinions throughout the United States. Some believe the Common Core is already prioritized, and feel strongly they must teach it all since it is all important. Others believe these views are unrealistic given the number of standards, the increased levels of rigor, the number of days in the year, and the need for students to master the skills to high levels of proficiency by the end of each school year. Which side are you more prone to agree with? Why?

CHAPTER SIX

Barstow Unified School District, San Bernardino County, California

"When Barstow Unified School District embraced the Common Core State Standards Initiative, we were fortunate to have developed a relationship with The Leadership and Learning Center to guide us in this process. Throughout our ongoing teacher training, The Leadership and Learning Center staff has empowered our teacher leaders in building the best lessons and environments for their classrooms by creating clear and realistic goals for student learning. With our continued relationship with The Leadership and Learning Center staff, we look forward to a smooth implementation of the Common Core State Standards in our district."

JEFF MALAN,
SUPERINTENDENT, BARSTOW USD

RCD District: Barstow Unified School District

Location: San Bernardino County, California (Rural)

Population: 5,991 students

Author: Teresa Healy, Assistant Superintendent, Educational Services

Who We Are

Barstow Unified School District is located in the heart of the High Desert midway between Los Angeles and Las Vegas, within San Bernardino County, California. Our geographically isolated community is home to Fort Irwin National Training Center, Marine Corps Logistics Base Barstow, and Burlington Northern Santa Fe Railroad; these are the major employers of this isolated, rural community. Barstow Unified School District has 5,991 students (declining growth) enrolled in eight elementary schools, one junior high school, one comprehensive high school, and one continuation high school. Of this number, 66 percent participate in the free and reduced lunch program, 11 percent are identified as special education, and 9 percent are enrolled in gifted and talented programs.

Barstow Unified School District is in "year 3+ of program improvement" under No Child Left Behind (NCLB) and has provided considerable professional development to all teachers to improve the instructional practices for students. Regular collaboration time is set aside each week for staff to discuss student performance, instructional strategies, and lesson design. Teacher instructional coaches worked with each of the teachers to implement and improve instructional practices on a one-on-one and small-group basis.

Barstow Unified School District Demographics:

	2009/10	2010/11	2011/12
Hispanic	47.8%	49.8%	51.5%
White	29.2%	27.4%	26.8%
African American	16.5%	14.8%	13.9%
Socioeconomically Disadvantaged	66.4%	68.0%	66.1%

Barstow Unified School District Standardized Testing and Reporting (STAR) Results:

	2009/10	2010/11	2011/12
Adequate Yearly Progress—ELA	47.1%	48.2%	50.4%
Adequate Yearly Progress—Math	47.5%	52.0%	55.1%
Academic Performance Index	707	734	747

How We Got to Rigorous Curriculum Design

When Barstow Unified School District was identified for "program improvement" under No Child Left Behind during the fall of 2008, we were assigned sanctions by the State of California that included utilizing the California State Board of Education-adopted basic core instructional programs and materials in reading/language arts (RLA)/English language development (ELD) and mathematics, including ancillary materials for universal access. These programs are to be implemented as designed and documented for daily use in every classroom, with materials provided for every student. Additionally, professional development to support this implementation was required of each teacher. As a result of this implementation, prescriptive, detailed pacing guides were put into place and administrative walkthroughs in classrooms were carried out to ensure compliance and effectiveness. Classrooms became more uniform as teachers used the adopted course materials with fidelity and utilized the instructional model of "direct interactive instruction," as directed by state sanctions.

In August 2010, the California State Board of Education adopted the Common Core State Standards. As a district, we watched as this process began to unfold, and attended county-sponsored awareness and introductory events to keep ourselves abreast of the latest information.

We soon realized that the Common Core State Standards were very different from our current state standards in terms of levels of rigor and expectations necessary for students to demonstrate mastery of the standards. We recognized that our current pacing guides and methods of instructing students would not be sufficient when we were required to assess students on their mastery of the Common Core State Standards.

We also learned from our NCLB program improvement experience how valuable it is to "get in front of" a problem, rather than languishing in the background and hoping that our students would somehow be successful in the new system, or waiting for others to set the pace and leave our students lagging behind.

As a district, we looked at the Common Core standards and recognized that we would need assistance with the transition, as we did not have enough expertise to do so on our own. We began to search with colleagues in other districts for vendors we had previously worked with to see who was "getting out ahead of the curve" to implement these new standards, and found out that most were taking a wait-and-see approach to this issue.

Coincidentally, we were working with Ed King, our Houghton Mifflin Harcourt instructional materials sales representative, to supplement some of our materials where we had identified needs for struggling students. In the conversation, it came up that the materials would be aligned to the CCSS. I asked the representative if he knew of any resources to help make the transition to the new standards. He shared information about The Leadership and Learning Center and many of their programs. We knew of The Center's reputation for quality and did some more homework about the Rigorous Curriculum Design process. Two principals and I attended The Leadership and Learning Center's "Common Core Summit" in Chicago in July, 2011, and heard Larry Ainsworth describe the RCD model. We really liked what we saw as a process for curriculum design and knew it would fit well into our district culture. We selected The Leadership and Learning Center's Rigorous Curriculum Design process for the following reasons:

- It allowed us to create a complete curriculum product to share with teachers that included prioritized standards, interim assessments, pacing plans, and unit design, all of which fit in with our current system and allowed us to take a step forward;

- RCD is a very collaborative process that works for all grade levels and subjects;

- The units of study include references to strong instructional practices that will enable us to maintain rigor for all of our students.

As a past practice, Barstow Unified School District had a "leadership academy" that met bimonthly, which included site principals, two teacher representatives from each site, and the district administration. This group did much of the visioning, planning, and implementing for our program improvement process. As the principals and I discussed the best way to implement the Rigorous Curriculum Design process with the Common Core State Standards, we decided to use a similar model, ensuring that we had representatives from each grade level in attendance. We started with the idea of including one teacher from each grade level at each site to increase buy-in to the process and product, but quickly realized that this was not feasible, as we have small schools and a substitute teacher shortage issue. Instead we settled on two teachers from each *site*, creating representatives for each grade level at the district meetings. Principals asked their strongest teachers to take part, explaining that they would need to be willing to put in the time and to be out of their classroom for all of the training dates. I made sure that we had two teacher representatives from each grade level—one for each subject area.

We scheduled each session approximately six weeks apart to allow the design teams to learn the specific steps of the process taught during the session and then complete the related task prior to the next session. Grade-level groups met outside of the sessions to complete tasks, in order to be ready to move on to the next step at the following session. We had to work around testing schedules, student breaks, and key instructional times, which made the scheduling a bit challenging. But we ended up with a workable schedule, spending about a year to complete the process.

As we began to schedule the professional development sessions, we realized we were putting quite a bit on the shoulders of our teachers in the design groups. I met with fellow assistant superintendents from neighboring districts to see if we could create a collaborative effort to learn the process, create units, and share best practices. As a result, two districts joined us in this process, sending teacher leaders to participate in the sessions and then to take the information back to their respective school districts and create their own units or to revise ours. This collaboration has been good for our district, as we are isolated geographically. In addition, it allowed all participants to have a much more in-depth conversation regarding each step and the resulting product. It also helped to create an environment where teachers were acknowledged as professionals having extensive backgrounds and expertise to share, lifting the conversations to a high level of competence.

We were fortunate to have Dr. Connie Kamm, a Senior Professional Development Associate with The Leadership and Learning Center, as our trainer throughout this process. Her experience in working with schools and particularly with the Rigorous Curriculum Design process has been invaluable in guiding us through the transition from the California Content Standards to the Common Core State Standards. She has guided us step-by-step, paced to our needs, provided current updates on the Common Core and the Smarter Balanced Assessment Consortium, and also offered insights and lessons learned from other schools and districts. We have completed nine of the 12 sessions scheduled and have completed at least one unit of work for both English language arts and math. Our sessions included:

- Reviewing in depth the new Common Core State Standards;

- Prioritizing these standards, and determining which were priority and which were supporting, and ensuring that there was continuity as students progressed from kindergarten to high school graduation;

- Identifying units of study for the entire school year and assigning the standards to these units, ensuring that all Priority Standards were given sufficient time and that *all* standards (priority and supporting) were included;

- Preparing a grade-specific pacing calendar to ensure that each unit was given sufficient instructional time and that it flowed throughout the school year;

- Revising the unit planning organizer to meet our specific needs and beginning to populate the documents (Figure 6.1, a blank sample unit plan organizer that we adapted from the RCD unit planners, is shown at the end of this chapter);

- "Unwrapping" the prioritized standards to identify the concepts, skills, and levels of rigor and then creating Essential Questions and corresponding Big Ideas;

- Creating common formative pre- and post-assessments for each unit that mirror the skills, levels of rigor, and concepts in the Common Core;

- Planning "engaging learning experiences" that include engaging scenarios, performance tasks, learning progressions, unit sequencing, instructional strategies and supporting activities, differentiation options, instructional resources, vocabulary lists, and focus wall supports as described by Connie Kamm: "Focus walls are a district-wide practice. Every classroom keeps outcomes for learning, vocabulary (content and academic words), and other unit-specific information posted in the classroom to support student learning. In the vocabulary section of Barstow's RCD unit planner, designers have included a focus wall link so that teachers will have the vocabulary words for that unit ready to print out and post on their focus walls."

Currently, the design groups have a unit completed, which we shared with teachers at our back-to-school professional development day in August 2012. During this time, the teachers received an overview of the Rigorous Curriculum Design process, Common Core standards, and SBAC tests. They then met in grade-level (elementary) or department (secondary) groups where the Rigorous Curriculum Design group teachers facilitated the session to review the process that occurred, share the completed unit they had created, and solicit peer feedback. We asked teachers to assist the design group by helping them develop the engaging scenario and performance tasks, and by "unwrapping" the standards for the next unit.

The Rigorous Curriculum Design teams will continue to meet regularly during this next school year to complete the remainder of the units. As each unit is completed, they will be shared electronically and also discussed at our district collaboration meetings each trimester. The unveiling of the newly developed units had caused some stress to the design team, but all of the units have been well received by the rest of the district's teachers and have led to valuable discussions.

We expect to have all of the units completed by the end of the 2012/13 school year so that we may begin using them during the 2013/14 school year in preparation for the Smarter Balanced Assessment Consortium assessments that will be first administered in 2014/15.

At the beginning of this process, we knew that extensive professional development would need to occur to support the implementation of the Common Core, in both unit design and instructional strategies and practices. The Rigorous Curriculum Design process has filled the need for the unit design portion, and we will work through our collaborative processes currently in place to continue to revise and improve the units as we implement them.

We will begin in spring of 2013 to work more closely with all of the district teachers to ensure that the units are shared and readied for implementation in the fall of 2013. Early-out collaboration time, led by the Rigorous Curriculum Design team teachers, will be imperative to ensure a positive beginning of the implementation. As we design the units, our instructional teacher coaches are making note of areas that will require professional development, but we are also aware that we will need to spend a significant amount of time working with all teachers on instructional strategies and assessment practices because the structure of what we expect students to know and be able to do, and how they will demonstrate this, will be very different. It is also apparent that we will need to provide content support to teachers to ensure that they have the background knowledge to best support student learning.

Our immediate next steps are:

- Completion of the full year of content units for all grade levels in both English language arts and math (Spring 2013);

- Effective dissemination of the completed units to all teachers (June 2013);

- Inclusion of science, history/social sciences, and elective teachers in this process to design units in their subject areas to support Common Core literacy standards (Spring 2013);

- Determination of course of action for professional development in content support and instructional practice transition (June 2013).

Our long-term next steps include:

- Provide professional development in content support and instructional practice transition (Summer 2013–Spring 2014);

- Offer initial instruction of units in all classrooms K–12 (2013/14);

- Revise the units as they are taught based on feedback from teachers, data collected, and updates from the Smarter Balanced Assessment Consortium (2013/14);

- Continue the coaching model to support teachers in implementing the instructional practices (2013–2016).

"It is a remarkable opportunity to be involved with the Rigorous Curriculum Design process for our district. The Common Core math standards are written to develop a deep knowledge of mathematical concepts and understanding rather than the explanation and follow up assignment process of the past and today. The engaging scenarios and learning tasks not only engage all students in the learning process, but also help to prepare them for the type of mathematical thinking they will need for ever-changing future workplaces. The units of study will help students work with numbers in a way that is not present in the current curriculum adoptions, by composing and decomposing numbers and representing them many different ways. Students will begin to use many strategies through the development of the Common Core's Standards for Mathematical Practice—over and above the standard algorithm. These developments will teach students to be forward thinkers and problem solvers, and to develop a quality of persistence and depth of knowledge so often lacking in the present generation. It is truly a privilege to be a teacher in this exciting time of change in the United States."

ROBIN NOWOTNY,
THIRD-GRADE TEACHER, CRESTLINE ELEMENTARY SCHOOL

Hard Work and Positive Changes

The Rigorous Curriculum Design process is tough work. The process causes teachers to think about what they are asking students to know and be able to do and how the students will demonstrate their learning. The Rigorous Curriculum Design process also requires that teachers ensure that there is a clear learning progression from grade level to grade level. This work requires that teachers engage in a deep level of conversation with colleagues, debate nuances in instruction and content, and come to a consensus on what is best for students. It also requires a high level of trust in our teachers' ability to develop a product that will help teachers to implement the Common Core standards at a level that is required. Throughout this process, I was able to observe and participate in these conversations of professional educators creating units that will be rigorous, interesting, and attainable for students. It has been an extraordinary experience.

"Rigorous Curriculum Design allows for teachers to participate in instructional conversations using dialectical reasoning to work

through cognitive dissonance and create highly effective authentic units of instruction that will assist teachers in effectively teaching the CCSS."

HEATHER REID,
ELEMENTARY ELA COACH, BARSTOW USD

The Center's Rigorous Curriculum Design process has created a true sense of collaboration among the team members. The collaborative process among teachers at different grade levels, school sites, and with members from other district teams was evident from the beginning as we prioritized the CCSS and ensured that there was a true learning progression from grade level to grade level in each strand.

The collaborative process was also evident as we revised the unit planning organizer multiple times to ensure that it is a consistently useful tool for all teachers in all subject areas. This collaborative process is also apparent as we do quality checks along the way, where design team members share their latest work for others to critique. Each step of writing the units involves collaboration, whether it is a grade-level pair working through the details of a unit or a nearby grade-level team offering suggestions when another team has writer's block. This spirit of camaraderie has also carried over to school sites as we work on other tasks.

As I shared earlier in this chapter, one of the reasons we chose to participate in the Rigorous Curriculum Design process to transition to the Common Core was to get out in front of the implementation and to give ourselves time to have an effective implementation of the new curriculum. Although sometimes we have wondered if we were moving along on the right route, there has also been a sense of empowerment in getting to determine the path that our students will take as they experience the curriculum. As a group we have established parameters in the curriculum, including performance tasks, assessment routines and items, and formats for delivering instruction.

An additional positive outcome has been the reaction from the rest of the district teachers. Whenever updates are shared by design team members, the feedback has been encouraging and constructive. I was at a county meeting where our teachers union president, who is not a design team member, was sharing how far ahead we were in implementing the Common Core standards and that it was due to the hard work of the committed educators on the design team and the district's choice to use the Rigorous Curriculum Design process.

Challenges

The Rigorous Curriculum Design process challenges teachers to think outside the box and really contemplate what the Common Core standards mean, what it looks like when students master them, and how best to get students to this level within the time constraints in which we all live. It was tempting to fall back to our old ways of just finding a standards correlation chart in our instructional materials and creating a pacing guide to go along with this. I heard many times during sessions, "We are not curriculum designers, we are teachers—isn't someone paid to do this work? Why can't we just wait for them to do it?" However, the work continued, and the same teachers who made these comments have since developed impressive units for students.

It was also a concern for the participating teachers, who were identified as being some of the best in the district and therefore some of the most conscientious, to be out of their classrooms for so many days. I constantly heard about the impact of having substitute teachers in classrooms, that there was a lack of continuity and a big dependency on neighboring teachers to ensure that lessons were being taught while design team teachers were out of classes. The group has met for three sessions in the summer and that has eased this concern substantially.

Another challenge was the idea that we might actually be too far ahead of California's Common Core standards implementation. We were writing common formative assessments and performance tasks with little knowledge of what the Smarter Balanced Assessment Consortium (SBAC) was going to require and how the tests would look. Had we selected the "right" Priority Standards? What if our tasks were too different or formatted differently? Were the SBAC assessments really going to have midterm assessments to measure students' progress against? Did we need to include this as well? Every time we heard a tidbit of information, we scrambled to make adjustments. We finally realized we needed to go with our guts, as grade-level and subject experts, and that we would make whatever adjustments were needed after we finished the units.

A concern that is also valid is how to create buy-in to this process and product for teachers who were not directly involved. The Director of Instructional Support and I visited each school site a few times during the year and did a "fireside chat" to share updates with the entire staff and to answer questions. We also encouraged principals during staff meetings to have their design team members share the progress and process with their faculty members. Hearing from a trusted colleague from their site has helped to ease teacher concern. Additionally, all of the work in progress was posted in a shared internal electronic folder so that all teachers could view and offer feedback on any of the documents. Keeping all of the teachers informed of the process and progress and providing a forum for feedback has eliminated much of the concern for the teachers.

One of our next steps is to work with the science, history/social studies, and elective teachers to create units in their subject areas to support the Common Core literacy standards. Having this group start behind the others was a conscious decision as we did not know what California would do with the current content standards or if the state would create new Common Core standards for those disciplines. It has impeded some conversations to coordinate efforts across departments, but in light of the fact that we only now have a draft of the CCSS for science, I believe it was a wise decision. We will begin to work with these departments in the fall and will share the current work from ELA and math at that time.

I am hoping that our list of challenges is not discouraging to others who are considering beginning this work. I believe that we can learn from each other and that to just share our successes and positive changes would not share a complete picture of the power of this process. As each challenge arose, we addressed it and continued to have the work go forward. Sharing our challenges will hopefully enable you to be prepared to answer some of these concerns when you begin the process in your own school district.

Reflections

As the Assistant Superintendent of Educational Services for Barstow USD, I feel that I need to know what our teachers are hearing and doing during any professional development sessions. I therefore attend and strive to help facilitate many of our professional development opportunities to ensure that there is a clear and consistent message and that any questions are answered as we go. Participating in the Rigorous Curriculum Design process has enabled me to watch our teachers process the learning and interpret it to the best advantage for our students.

As the design groups learn a task and work to complete it, the levels of discussion, the debate about what students can and cannot do, and the discussion of the learning progressions as we move from grade level to grade level creating engaging scenarios and performance tasks have been nothing short of amazing. The work is intensive, but well worth the effort. The work products are well on their way to becoming an important tool for teachers to utilize to improve student learning. I wish that I could share that sense of the intensity of the work with all of you who are reading these pages—that itself was worth the effort of putting this professional development together to create a very worthwhile experience for all. I am looking forward to taking the next steps in our process and observing the units in action with students—a great product that will get our students where they need to be: successful!

FIGURE 6.1 **Barstow Unified School District RCD Unit Plan Organizer**

Subject(s)	
Grade/Course	
Unit of Study	
Duration of Unit	

Priority Standards

Supporting Standards

"Unwrapped" Concepts (students need to know)	"Unwrapped" Skills (students need to be able to do)	Bloom's Taxonomy Levels

Essential Questions	Corresponding Big Ideas

FIGURE
6.1 **Barstow Unified School District RCD Unit Plan Organizer** *(continued)*

Standardized Assessment Correlations (State, College and Career)	
(Future Reference to SBAC/Career College Assessments)	
Unit Assessments	
Pre-Assessment	**Post-Assessment**
Scoring Guides/Answer Keys/Rationale	

Unit Vocabulary Terms/Glossary/Focus Walls

Engaging Scenario

Authentic Performance Tasks	Engaging Learning Experiences Synopses of Authentic Performance Tasks	Suggested Length of Time
Task 1		
Task 2		
Task 3		
Task 4		

Authentic Performance Task 1—(Title) Length: ____ days		
Standards Addressed in Authentic Performance Task 1		

Priority:

Supporting:

FIGURE 6.1 **Barstow Unified School District RCD Unit Plan Organizer** *(continued)*

Objectives

Description of Authentic Performance Task 1	Bloom's Taxonomy Levels

Link to Task Planner:	
Scoring Guide for Authentic Performance Task 1 (Insert link to document)	

Instructional Strategies and Supporting Activities for Authentic Peformance Task 1 (Include vocabulary strategy)	Differentiated Accommodations and Modifications Including Strategies for English Language Learners (Vary content, process, product)	Differentiated Enrichment/ Extensions Modifications	Resources and Materials (e.g., technical tools, graphic organizers, simulations, multimedia sources, print and non-print materials)

Interdisciplinary Connections

Getting Started on Your Journey

As you reflect on Barstow Unified School District's experience, think about how their story applies to you in your current setting, and then answer the following questions:

1. *At the beginning of this process, we knew that extensive professional development would need to occur to support the implementation of the Common Core, in both unit design and instructional strategies and practices.*

   What types of professional development (workshops, conferences, even reading) have you engaged in regarding the Common Core? Is your entire school or system participating in this professional development with you, or are you learning individually and/or in smaller teams? What critical learnings have resulted from this professional development?

2. *A concern that is also valid is how we create buy-in to this process and product for teachers who were not directly involved. The Director of Instructional Support and I visited each school site a few times during the year and did a "fireside chat" to share updates with the entire staff and to answer questions. We also encouraged principals during staff meetings to have their design team members share the progress and process with their faculty members. Hearing from a trusted colleague from their site has helped to ease teacher concern.*

   Creating buy-in for any new initiative is always a concern for leaders. How much buy-in do you believe is necessary to begin and then sustain implementation of a new initiative? Who are the essential stakeholders that must be on board?

   Think of a recent initiative you have started implementing. What have you done to generate buy-in?

3. *As the Assistant Superintendent of Educational Services for Barstow USD, I feel that I need to know what our teachers are hearing and doing during any professional development sessions. I therefore attend and strive to help facilitate many of our professional development opportunities to ensure that there*

is a clear and consistent message and that any questions are answered as we go. Participating in the Rigorous Curriculum Design process has enabled me to watch our teachers process the learning and interpret it to the best advantage for our students.

For those in leadership roles, it can be particularly challenging to free up time in demanding schedules for those things that are important but not urgent. If you are a leader in your school or district, have you been able to carve out time to learn alongside those you lead to ensure you are knowledgeable regarding the ins and outs of the implementation of key initiatives? If you aren't a school or district leader, do those who lead you take the time to learn with you? What impact do these actions have on those in your setting?

CHAPTER SEVEN

Hemet Unified School District, Riverside County, California

"Our teams understood that in order to meet the needs of our 21st-century learners, and the demands of the Common Core State Standards, we needed to do what we had not done before. No longer would we work in grade-level/discipline isolation and follow a lockstep program. We were going to design curricular units of study that thoughtfully and strategically placed all the pieces together."

DAVID HORTON and TRACY CHAMBERS

RCD District: Hemet Unified School District, Valley Central School District

Location: Riverside County, California (Suburban and Rural)

Population: Approximately 22,000 students

Authors: David Horton, Ed.D., Director of Accountability, and Tracy Chambers, Director of Professional Development

Demographics

Hemet Unified School District (HUSD) covers one of the largest geographic areas of any district in California, with more than 700 square miles of very diverse topography from valley flatlands, to foothills, to mountains. For several years our demographics have changed as the numbers of Hispanic students, English language learners, and children living in poverty steadily increase.

Hemet is 49 percent Hispanic, 37 percent white, and 8 percent African American. Fifteen percent of our students are English language learners, 73 percent are socioeconomically disadvantaged, and 13 percent are in special education. We maintain a staff of nearly 1,000 teachers, counselors, and psychologists, 67 certificated management employees, and 1,760 classified employees. These adults, plus approximately 22,000 students, fill nine preschool centers, 11 elementary schools (K–5), three elementary/middle schools (K–8), four middle schools (6–8), four comprehensive high schools (9–12), one continuation high school (9–12), one adult education center, one alternative education program, one independent study program, one middle school charter, and one high school charter.

Background

For many years, Hemet Unified School District, undoubtedly like many districts, found itself steeped in all things No Child Left Behind (NCLB). Over time, dealing with NCLB became more of a process in reactivity rather than proactivity. We responded to instructional issues by looking for the one "silver bullet" that would fix everything related to teaching and leading students, so we purchased this program, that professional development, some fairly nifty software. Although well intentioned, the initiatives we adopted eventually created a pile-up and resulted in "initiative fatigue." They left our administrators, and worse still our teachers, in a guessing game as to what it is they should really be using or working on to support student learning; this fostered stress and frustration. We really didn't have a cohesive and clear plan to unify our path with curriculum, assessment, and instruction. Each initiative became an island unto itself, and we continually looked for the next best thing to solve our issues. We found ourselves running faster and faster to support and implement initiative after initiative, only to discover we were just adding another coat of paint to a broken and splintered fence.

Our professional development struggled to keep pace with our fractured focus. We began to look for ways to build capacity of people instead of allowing sites to choose their own path. One of the capacity-building initiatives that we put in place was a focus on professional learning communities (PLCs). In the early stages we had scattered pockets of schools and teams marching off to trainings. They would come back excited but soon found themselves bogged down in the mountain of other initiatives they were trying to grapple with.

Our data management systems were also in a very fractured place. Due to several programs and grants, we were using two different systems to track student data. This proved both confusing and divisive. Some people became very stuck with one system and shunned the other and vice versa. This created a nightmare when striving to provide professional development and cohesive usage policies.

We lived a "fidelity to the core" lifestyle. We continually pushed and harped on the need to be lockstep and rigid with our curriculum execution in classrooms. Little by little, over each successive year, we seemed to achieve the goal of having entire grade levels/disciplines on the same page of the book on the same day. We found, of course, that this left little room for the individual needs of students, and even though we knew this in the back of our minds, we continued to live in a pacing guide/textbook-driven world. We operated in the space that if only all the teachers would march to the same beat at exactly the same time, in exactly the same way, then surely we would achieve the results we sought. Sadly, year after year, we moved closer to the target of a highly lockstep teaching staff but our student achievement only moved along at a modest pace, never setting the world on fire with large bursts of improvement.

This reactive model left us continually trying to rearrange the deck chairs on a ship that was slowly sinking. We had problems in the engine room and with the architecture of the ship. It really didn't matter if the tablecloths in the dining hall matched and the place settings were immaculate. It was a losing battle. We were burning out at both the teacher level and the administrative level. Something had to give. All of our energy was spent reactively feeding the high-stakes accountability machine, with little success, and the iceberg was looming in the darkness.

The Move to Data Teams

Our experience in Hemet Unified School District could easily be summed up by saying we were "data-rich and information-poor." We had plenty of data, in multiple places, but it was never used to determine what teachers would do differently to teach students in a more informed way and therefore improve their performance. The idea of data-based decision making sounded really nice, but we were spinning around in such a reactive fashion it began to feel as though nothing we were doing would ever make a profound difference.

In the spring of 2010, two administrators began the journey of helping the district right the ship when they attended The Leadership and Learning Center's two-day workshop on Data Teams (DT) and Decision Making for Results (DMR). Their enthusiasm for the content, and how it would dramatically improve their PLCs, quickly spread from the seminar, and a commitment was made for them to attend the three-day certification training. The message from these trainings quickly became the focus of several conversations at the district level. From there, the decision was made that all sites would participate in, and focus deeply on, Data Teams training and would establish instructional Data Teams in grade levels and content areas.

The first year (2010/11) of Data Teams training for administrators took place in small doses. We strategically broke down the high points of DMR and delivered these pieces in our monthly leadership meetings for principals. By the time the school year was over in June, we were able to deliver the first day of the two-day DMR/DT training to all administrators. We set the expectation that at the start of the new school year (2011/12) all schools would be expected to have Data Teams in place and functioning by the sixth week of school.

When we started the 2011/12 school year we used one day of our "welcome back symposium" to deliver the second day of DMR/DT training. Our next step was to get our professional development coaches trained in DMR/DT. The coaches' role in this "roll-out" year was to support individual Data Teams at sites.

From the district level, we set several expectations to get Data Teams off the ground. One was that each site was to have a data wall to publicly display the progress of each team. We also created a district data wall to showcase the data most indicative of our district focus and achievements. We required that at elementary sites grades 2–5, at minimum, be involved in Data Teams. Middle schools were required to have math and English language arts (ELA) Data Teams. High schools were to have math and ELA Data Teams functioning in at least algebra I, geometry, and ninth- and tenth-grade English language arts.

During the 2011/12 school year, we expanded the reach of the Data Teams significantly. We trained our first set of lead teachers in Data Teams from each school site in spring 2012. We also were able to send all of our professional development team members plus several administrators to be certified in DMR/DT in spring 2012. Our goal with this cadre of staff is to provide a more formal training and support network for a deeper roll-out of DMR/DT in the 2012/13 school year.

A major area of need surfaced early in our Data Teams roll-out. We did not have time set aside for our Data Teams to meet. It was costing us a great deal of money in the 2011/12 school year to provide release-time substitutes to allow teachers the time to meet as Data Teams. This was, of course, not optimal. All of that time out of classrooms was not our first choice. To try and mitigate the situation, we began a collaborative conversation with our teachers union executive board to talk about how we could set aside collaboration time for all schools on one day in the week.

To assist the executive board in better understanding what we were doing as a district, we invited them to attend two seminars by The Leadership and Learning Center. The first was on the Common Core. The second focused on a study of 90/90/90 schools (schools with 90 percent of students eligible for free or reduced lunch, 90 percent ethnic minorities, and 90 percent achieving the district or state academic standards in reading or another area). Both events helped a great deal to give us a common frame of reference as to where we were headed as a district. With careful planning, we were able to enter into a memorandum of understanding with our teachers union to have "late-start Tuesdays." This change in schedule will give us much needed time for our teachers to meet and have the regular rich conversations that will move their Data Teams forward in even greater ways.

Rigorous Curriculum Design

As we moved through our second year of Data Teams implementation, we started to receive feedback from teams across the district, and we had some serious areas of concern. One glaring need was getting our curriculum to align seamlessly in a Data Teams environment. The "timing" we used to teach units of study was pacing guide/textbook driven rather than standard/topic driven. This rigidity in the schedule created a disconnect and barrier for the educators who were trying to teach and monitor student progress in a Data Teams setting—they didn't have the time or permission to address the authentic needs of the learners they were trying to teach as the next skill was always calling.

Another need rose to the top, and that was the push to get an organized roll-out of the Common Core State Standards in place. We started attending trainings and having executive discussions about how we envisioned getting these standards into the hands of our teachers in advance of the new assessments coming in 2015. We couldn't come to a definitive conclusion as to how we wanted to uniformly get these standards in place. Also factoring into our CCSS conversation was trying to figure out how to navigate the "new world" of Common Core curricula while using "old-world" textbooks. Given the condition of the state budget in California, we realized that we may not see updated textbooks aligned to the Common Core for at least three to five years.

Finally, we felt a continued pressure to move our curriculum and instruction firmly into the 21st century. In other words, we regularly saw the need to provide an education for our students that truly engages and prepares them for either college or career. Recognizing that our system was not well structured to accomplish this led us to have conversations about what pieces were missing or preventing us from truly getting students as prepared as possible for our ever-changing world. These conversations regularly focused on the strategies our teachers used, as well as the resources that were available, that could empower them to both engage and instruct students in a 21st-century style.

During a district certification training in Data Teams, we were shown a sample of a Rigorous Curriculum Design unit created by The Leadership and Learning Center. After conducting more questioning, study, and networking about this RCD sample, many saw this process of unit planning as the potential solution we were looking for to address 21st-century learning, Common Core State Standards implementation and assessment, and the curricular pacing issues through the Data Teams cycle. Rigorous Curriculum Design soon became the focus of a very high-level collaborative conversation at the district level. The more we studied RCD, and examined our issues, the more we knew that engaging in this powerful model was the only answer.

We officially launched into planning for Rigorous Curriculum Design success by adopting a simple structure for our roll-out. We talked about the "who, what, when, where, and how" in order to get the basic logistics underway. One key question we asked in this early phase was: "Where do we want to be 6, 12, 24, and 36 months from now?" We forced ourselves to imagine not just the product and changed teacher practice that would result from the RCD work, but also how/where we would house it, how we would distribute the plans, train people, obtain feedback and constructive criticism on the units, and how we would monitor and evaluate the administration of the units in the classrooms. In other words, if Rigorous Curriculum Design was the answer, then how would we implement it *well, deeply,* and *over time* in every school and classroom?

Part one of our planning was set aside to address the "what." Our first consideration was to determine what subject areas we were going to target initially. Given the rigor of the Common Core and the corresponding new assessments, we decided to narrow our focus and begin with math and ELA (K–12) in phase 1. We have already made plans to bring science and social science into the RCD process in 2013/14. Then, finally, we will bring elective disciplines into RCD in 2014/15.

We talked at length to ensure everything we did in the unit planning process could be done in an expandable digital format. We knew we had to build everything in digital templates that could grow to house more links and content over time, and make the units even richer as feedback and resources funneled in. We wanted our product to be a living, breathing document, so we decided to build in a feedback vetting system, to not only allow our educators to make constructive critiques of the units, but to also add resources, teaching ideas, hints, tips, instructional strategy ideas, Data Team connections, formative and summative assessment examples, and performance tasks/common scoring guides over time.

Next, we decided "who" our unit planning process would include. We knew going into Rigorous Curriculum Design that we needed a broad range of teaching experiences to be represented on the design team. We also wanted to include a representative from every school in the district, and specifically add special education representatives and "educational options" school representatives to the group. Our intention was to have the RCD units built with all schools and all students in mind, so that every teacher would have a toolbox that works for them in their own setting, relevant to their particular students and specific needs.

We then petitioned principals to nominate two or three math and ELA teachers from their site. After the names were submitted, we met as a district team, that included professional development coaches, to talk about the chemistry of each team and to be sure each grade level had at least two representatives on it. We were intentional about ensuring a balance between very experienced veteran teachers and relatively new teachers, every one of them being the top recommendation of their principal or a district staff member. By the time the selection process was over we had more than 50 of the very best teachers in our district. We then split them into two RCD design teams—one for math and one for ELA.

A major driver for us to move to the RCD units was the shift to the Common Core in math and ELA as well as the coming Smarter Balanced assessment in the spring of 2015. Knowing the assessment would be a reality in a very few years, this gave us our "when." Now we were ready to plan the roll-out and implementation targets accordingly.

We started work on the initial unit plans in the spring of 2012 with a target completion of fall 2012. We figured this would give us until the spring of 2013 to pilot the units, and then use the remainder of the time to work out the bugs, smooth out our systems, and get the feedback loops in full working order. We are targeting the 2013/14 school year as our year to have the Rigorous Curriculum Design units on the ground and in all teachers' hands, and ensure they are trained and ready to go. If all goes as planned, we will be in year two of our implementation when the first Common Core assessments arrive on the scene.

We scheduled all of our training at our district office—this is the "where." We are fortunate to have space large enough for all 50 teachers, 26 principals, and about 20 district administrators plus invited guests to attend our opening two-day RCD training. We used these two days as a chance to provide one uniform message about what the RCD process is about. In other words, we wanted all the key players to have a common vocabulary, a common direction, and an understanding of not only where we are going but why we are going there.

Now we needed to consider "how" we would implement well and deeply. We had several district-level conversations about how to allocate the resources to sustain this RCD process. Once we get the process started and complete units for math and ELA, we will be able to use coaches and other trained teachers to lead the process for our other subject areas. In other words, we expect to build and utilize our internal capacity to lead this work after our initial successful models with math and ELA have been created with support from The Leadership and Learning Center. In looking at the "how," another big consideration for us has been how to digitally store and transmit the RCD units to teachers both during the process and after the units are completed, and who will be designated as responsible for adding digital resources to units.

Approaching this process in a slow, methodical manner to begin with will allow for increased speed later. As the saying goes, "go slow to go fast." Our advice to other school systems beginning this process is to ask all the systemic questions and discuss all contingencies well in advance of implementation, to ensure that the powerful work you begin heads in the direction you desire it to go.

Challenges

As with any change process, challenges were, and continue to be, anticipated along the way. One of the largest obstacles we had to overcome was simply not being aware of many other districts traveling down the path of both the California Common Core standards and Rigorous Curriculum Design. As an educational services team, we had to meet regularly to discuss and anticipate the possible domino effect each decision would have on the organization as a whole.

As we continue to move toward completing the RCD instructional units, we work together as an educational services team to plan for ongoing communication, training, and implementation. We anticipate that one hurdle we will have to overcome as we move further along in the process is the lockstep programming we have indoctrinated our teachers with over the last eight years. The textbook has been the driving force behind the curriculum, instruction, and assessment in our classrooms. It will take time, training, and ongoing professional development to support our teaching staff in implementing the curricular units, and empowering them to use prioritized and "unwrapped" standards to be the driving force *in place of* the textbook. We anticipate this change will require tremendous resources (time, finances, and tools) to encourage teachers to creatively support one another as they discuss and find high-quality methods to deliver these RCD units.

The *ongoing* challenge we will continue to address is ensuring that we are monitoring every step of the process. For most of our staff this is a new way of approaching teaching and learning. As the process unfolds, the feelings of uncertainty will begin to settle in, and we know that what we monitor, people pay attention to. The challenge becomes to make sure there are open lines of communication and feedback mechanisms in place to support everyone along this journey.

Positive Changes

As the energy and excitement began to grow among the educational services team members, one variable still remained: How would our teachers react to the process? In other words, how ready are we to radically change how we deliver curriculum and instruction to our students? These questions were unanswered until the completion of the second day of our RCD seminar. The Leadership and Learning Center facilitators, Rachel Syrja and Paul Bloomberg, took our RCD design teams through an activity that asked them to share how they felt about embarking on this process. This was the "bare your soul" moment. One response after another highlighted the sense of excitement, empowerment, and creativity the educators on the RCD design teams felt. Some of the quotes were: "We are ready to take the bull by the horns," "Our kids need more than the status quo and we are ready to develop an amazing curriculum," and "This process allows us to bring our wide range of experiences together."

Our teams understood that in order to meet the needs of our 21st-century learners, and the demands of the Common Core State Standards, we needed to do what we had not done before. No longer would we work in grade-level/discipline isolation and follow a lockstep program. We were going to design curricular units of study that thoughtfully and strategically placed all the pieces together. The double bonus was having the plan built to also seamlessly connect to our Data Teams work.

In Summary

Rigorous Curriculum Design combined with Data Teams has filled in the missing puzzle pieces as we seek to provide our students with a high-quality instructional delivery system. It is clear we have started on a very exciting journey. We will no longer operate in a reactive manner, but rather take a proactive approach to increasing student achievement. Along the way we are excited to see how Data Teams and RCD will begin to permeate into other aspects of our organization. In a very short period of time, we have seen a change in the culture and climate of the teachers and staff involved in the creation of the RCD units. This has already led to conversations about aligning our grading system and report cards to this process. We are also discussing how we may be able to align our teacher and administrative evaluations with the components of this grand initiative.

Our path into Rigorous Curriculum Design is likely not too different from how others have done it, how others are doing it, or how others will do it. We approached this effort more as a "connect the dots" effort than a "throw the baby out with the bath-water" effort. Meaning, we knew we had plenty of collective strengths. We also knew that we had some potholes and situations in need of attention. But, instead of scratching everything, we took the mindset that we could build on the good things we were already doing and grow from there. We have many great teachers with tremendous skill sets that lend themselves to this type of work. We harnessed these strengths, and fully expect they will be the skilled experts who will help drive this process exactly where it needs to go. Our end mission with both the RCD work as well as the Data Teams process is to have both empowering processes (not silver bullets) be *teacher-driven* and, eventually, *administrator-independent*.

Hemet Unified School District has learned through experience that the "quick fix" solutions rarely, if ever, work. Instead we have shifted to realizing that exceptional teaching, learning, and leadership is both a process and a journey, not a destination point. We know that we have to stay the course, keep our focus narrow, and continue to keep Rigorous Curriculum Design at the heart of the instructional decisions we make. We are excited to see the results this process will have for our students in preparing them for the 21st century.

Getting Started on Your Journey

As you reflect on Hemet Unified School District's methodology, think about how their story applies to you in your current setting, and then answer the following questions:

1. Can you relate to the scattered approach of addressing standards, assessment, instruction, professional development, data analysis, and implementation that the authors discuss at the beginning of their chapter?

   We found ourselves running faster and faster to support and implement initiative after initiative, only to discover we were just adding another coat of paint to a broken and splintered fence.

   > On a scale of one to 10, 10 being the highest degree of alignment possible, how would you rate your cohesiveness in the relationship between standards, assessment, instruction, professional development, data analysis, and implementation in your school or district? Explain.

2. Throughout the chapter, it is clear the district leadership was willing to make some tough decisions and walk down some difficult paths in order to make the changes their schools needed. One instance that clearly showed the district's tenacity and commitment was their efforts in working with the union to carve out weekly time for their Data Teams to meet.

   With careful planning we were able to enter into a memorandum of understanding with our teachers union to have "late-start Tuesdays." This change in schedule will give us much needed time for our teachers to meet and have the regular rich conversations that will move their Data Teams forward in even greater ways.

   > What are some of the other changes that were either inferred or stated in Hemet's story?

   > Has your school or district leadership also engaged in this type of courageous decision making in order to dramatically move teacher practice and increase student achievement? Explain.

3. The authors of this chapter walked us through their "who, what, when, where, and how" planning structure for implementation of Rigorous Curriculum Design. This simple, but highly effective scaffolding set the stage for deep implementation of this one initiative.

    Take time to think about one of the initiatives your school or district has committed to. What could be done to improve the planning, and therefore the sustainability, of this important practice?

CHAPTER EIGHT

Guilford County Schools, Guilford County, North Carolina

"The process was a roller-coaster ride because we really didn't know what was expected in the very beginning. Previously our units were more topical than conceptual. We no longer have any novel studies in the sixth grade. We had to redefine what is meant by 'text' and that has an impact on developing our units. Real-world assessments will take the place of quizzes and tests. That will be a real change!"

REBECCA MCKNIGHT,
GRADE 6 ELA TEACHER LEADER AND UNIT WRITER

RCD District: Guilford County Schools

Location: Guilford County, North Carolina (Urban)

Population: 72,000 students

Author: LeeAnn Segalla, Executive Director

Demographics

Guilford County Schools (GCS) is the third largest school system in North Carolina. The county is located in the middle of the state and includes Greensboro and High Point. The 122 schools serve approximately 72,000 students. The students speak 123 languages and dialects; 41 percent of the population is African American, 38 percent is white, and 11 percent is Hispanic. Students who qualify for free or reduced lunch represent 57 percent of the students. Preliminary reports for 2012 reflect that the district had an 85 percent graduation rate and 76 percent proficiency rate on the end-of-year tests.

Getting Started with the Common Core and RCD

In March 2011 The Leadership and Learning Center was contracted to introduce the Common Core to the English language arts (ELA) and mathematics curriculum specialists in the departments of curriculum and instruction, English as a second language (ESL), academically gifted (AG), and formative assessment. Over the next year, the ELA and math curriculum specialists attended full-day meetings each month with Center facilitators Connie Kamm and Lori Cook in Rigorous Curriculum Design. Through these monthly meetings they developed a deep understanding of the Common Core standards. ESL and AG specialists attended most of the math learning sessions but were only represented in a few of the ELA sessions. The formative assessment team participated in subject-area sessions when assessment was the topic of instruction. It should be noted that this chapter refers to curriculum design work completed in math and ELA. However, the same processes were also applied to science, social studies, health/PE, world languages, and the arts. All subjects were addressing new state standards. Rigorous Curriculum Design was the consistent framework used across all subjects and grades as a means of addressing the new state standards.

All curriculum specialists were engaged in providing professional development on Common Core standards to schools as they were learning. Some of the specialists also served as coaches in the district's most challenged schools. They had varied levels of experience in curriculum design. Most were novices at curriculum writing but all had been accomplished teachers who had written their own units for years. A few had completed extensive training with the "Understanding by Design" model of Grant Wiggins and Jay McTighe. However, only one math and one ELA curriculum specialist were on staff in the curriculum and instruction department during the previous North Carolina curriculum revision, and leadership in the department had also changed.

The elementary principals expressed interest in leading this curriculum change in their schools. The curriculum facilitator at each elementary school joined the principals for monthly sessions with the district curriculum specialists that were then replicated with their faculty at the individual school sites. In addition, each elementary school identified a teacher leader for each grade for mathematics and one for ELA. The teacher leaders attended three half-day sessions that provided additional details about Common Core standards and Rigorous Curriculum Design. Following the sessions, teacher leaders were responsible for sharing what they learned in the sessions with their grade level in professional learning communities. Therefore, each elementary school was learning as a whole faculty and as grade levels. Since there was a transition curriculum for math during 2011/12, the elementary curriculum specialists presented math the first semester and ELA during the second semester.

Middle and high schools used a different model. Each middle school selected one teacher leader for ELA and one teacher leader per grade (6, 7, and 8) for math. High schools selected one teacher leader per grade span 9–10 and 11–12 for math and one per grade span for ELA. The middle and high school teacher leaders met with the curriculum specialists one day monthly during 2011/12. Principals and curriculum facilitators in middle and high schools were provided abbreviated informational sessions at their monthly meetings.

The Work Begins

magine, the math and ELA curriculum specialist teams had different experiences as they engaged in this work. Both groups began by "un-Common Core standards. They used the revised Bloom's Taxonomy pth of Knowledge to identify the level of thinking skills for each standepts and skills were identified and written as "I can" statements in ...-menuly language. This led the way to identifying Priority Standards and their corresponding supporting standards. These steps were taken with previous curricula but they were predominately completed by curriculum specialists and provided to schools through the district's online curriculum management system, Guilford Education Management System (GEMS). GEMS is the repository for teaching and learning resources in Guilford County Schools. The curriculum specialists planned to replicate these processes with principals, curriculum facilitators, and teacher leaders during the first quarter of 2011.

Then curriculum specialist teams developed learning progressions in each discipline to illustrate how concepts and skills develop over time. The learning progressions would be an important tool as teachers provide scaffolding for struggling learners and extensions for students who learn quickly.

So far, so good. The work was tedious, but all of the curriculum specialists saw value in this work and, for the first time, the results would be consistent across both disciplines. After all, this wasn't that much different from the way the district provided past state curriculum revisions. They designed and prepared professional development for schools beginning with the July leadership conference and continuing through the first quarter. Held in late July 2011, the leadership conference featured a keynote session for principals and district administrators about the magnitude of change and leadership needed to implement the Common Core. Administrators were on board and supportive but remained apprehensive about the amount of work required to bring staff up to date.

The Chief Academic Officer and the Chief of Curriculum and Organization Development saw a "curricular sea change" that required more curricular support for teachers than ever before. The implementation of the Common Core and North Carolina Essential State Standards provided an opportunity for the school system to evaluate its curriculum management system and implement a design system that was consistent across grades and subjects. While components of Rigorous Curriculum Design were evident in the Guilford education management system (GEMS), there was a lack of coherent design and comprehensive curricular support. Figure 8.1 illustrates a comparison of the components of Rigorous Curriculum Design and the evidence of them in the GCS curriculum that is available to all staff on GEMS.

The need for a consistent unit template was clear.

The specialists set a goal of completing and posting on GEMS the following components before their winter break:

- K–12 unit template that would be used across disciplines;
- "Unwrapped" standards;
- Learning progressions;
- Identified Priority Standards and supporting standards;
- Standards clustered in teachable "chunks";
- Draft pacing guides;
- Academic vocabulary;
- One completed exemplar unit per grade, per subject (grade span for 9–10 and 11–12).

The main goal was to complete one exemplar unit and then teach teachers how to write the remaining units.

FIGURE 8.1 RCD and Guilford Education Management System (GEMS)

Rigorous Curriculum Design Component	GEMS
Learning theory or thinking skills taxonomy	None
Learning progressions	Few
Priority/Power Standards	Most
"Unwrapped" standards	Most
Pacing guide	Most
Essential Questions (RCD had a different purpose and meaning)	Some
Big Ideas	None
Unit title	None
Identified vocabulary	Most
Engaging scenarios	None
Pre- and Post-assessments	None
Instructional strategies	Most
Correlations of the standards to teacher and student resources	Most
Formative assessments	None
Scoring guides/performance rubrics	None
Differentiation strategies for English language learners, struggling learners, and advanced and gifted students	None
Lesson plan design	Some
Feedback process for users (teachers)	None
Vetting process for teacher writers	None

The summer and first quarter of the 2011/12 school year was a time of struggle, assimilation, and conflict for curriculum specialists as the work continued on unit development. It brought new meaning to the term "cognitive dissonance."

> *"The training was good, but I had trouble reconciling the concept-based training I already had from Lynn Erickson with Larry Ainsworth's design. It took me a couple of sessions to wrap my head around this new model," said a middle school ELA teacher.*

The elementary ELA team had particular difficulty integrating the reading foundational skills into the unit design. Curriculum specialists searched for an exemplar from another district and could not find one that reflected foundational reading skills instruction in a balanced literacy framework. It became very difficult for the kindergarten through second-grade ELA team to begin developing meaningful Rigorous Curriculum Design units. They wrestled with the long-range plan for implementing balanced literacy that was already underway, reading assessments that were relatively new, and the lack of sufficient instructional materials to implement the new Common Core curriculum. The pending professional development was looming on the horizon. As a first step, they had to create a sequence for teaching foundational standards. Then, as pacing guides and units began to take shape, the foundational standards were sufficiently integrated into the units.

In the meantime, the math curriculum specialists struggled with a unit template that worked for K–12. Their concepts of engaging scenarios were different. The high school team was worried about how the math teacher leaders were going to respond to this magnitude of change. The teachers had not used engaging scenarios and performance tasks as they are structured in Rigorous Curriculum Design.

Once the unit focus and primary concepts or skills were identified and the standards were clustered, the curriculum teams were able to develop pacing guides and write Big Ideas and the corresponding Essential Questions easily. All were keenly aware, however, that the Essential Questions that were currently posted in most Guilford County Schools classrooms did not serve the required purpose in the Rigorous Curriculum Design model. GCS teachers were accustomed to posting the lesson focus, or "I can …" statements for students, as Essential Questions, rather than the open-ended, overarching, and provocative questions used in the new model. Specialists realized that they needed to explicitly address this change in the role that Essential Questions play during their professional development with teachers and curriculum facilitators.

GCS has a formative assessment team whose members are experts at writing quarterly benchmark assessments and analyzing and interpreting assessment data with schools. Although the pre- and post-assessments in the math and ELA units were in a very different format, it was clear that these individuals could make a great contribution to the units. Pre- and post-assessments are written before any performance tasks, so the timing of this work was critical to maintaining a work schedule. Since the formative assessment team did not report to the curriculum and instruction leadership, they did not all have the same understanding of the unit design or sense of urgency for their contribution. Some saw it as one more responsibility for an already overworked staff. In the end, the formative assessment team provided outstanding pre- and post-assessments for the first unit. They will continue to make contributions to all of the units that are developed. These assessments and their corresponding scoring guides set a high standard for the quality of work that is consistent in the units.

For the first time, Guilford County Schools have specific scoring guides and rubrics that address all of the standards in math and ELA in every grade. This provides an opportunity for a truly standards-based system. The same learning standards and performance rubrics are provided system-wide, so no matter which GCS school a student attends, the same performance standards are set. The learning progressions served as a good tool as the performance rubrics were created. Great care was given to align the performance rubrics with the standards as well as the performance tasks.

> *"We've heard 'plan with the end in mind' for years. Now we have curricula that are actually written that way," said a sixth-grade teacher.*

Keep in mind that elementary schools were learning about Common Core standards and Rigorous Curriculum Design through monthly meetings with principals, curriculum facilitators, and teacher leaders, as well as in each grade and subject. The elementary curriculum specialists realized that it was unreasonable for the elementary teacher leaders to be able to write an entire unit by the end of the three half-day sessions and that principals and curriculum facilitators were learning new curriculum for two disciplines. As much as they wanted school staff to be part of the curriculum writing, the curriculum specialists realized that they were going be the ones writing the first unit of study in order to meet the deadline. Teacher writers would be employed in the summer of 2012 to write additional units in both disciplines.

Teacher leaders in grades 6–12, however, began working in small groups to develop one unit each since they were meeting for a full day almost every month. Each group of teacher leaders became part of a writing team so that all of the units for the grade or grade span could be written simultaneously. Curriculum specialists wrote the first unit and used it to model the writing process, targeting specific components for each meeting. For example, one session was devoted to writing engaging scenarios, so the curriculum specialists modeled how to write that component. All groups were then challenged to write engaging scenarios for the unit they were developing.

The curriculum specialists on the elementary math team truly collaborated on the unit development. They collectively reviewed the unit template and each specialist identified the parts to which he or she could make the greatest contribution. For example, one team member was particularly adept at writing engaging scenarios, another was a real sleuth at finding instructional resources, and still another was particularly strong with writing the details of the performance tasks. This strategy worked amazingly well for this team and resulted in very efficient use of their time.

As teams wrote units, the level of detail in the performance tasks was very high. The units were designed in an online format. Instructional strategies for each task were carefully selected to align with the standard, and links for more explicit examples of the strategies are embedded in the unit. Online resources for teachers and students are only a click away.

The units were sent to specialists in the English as a second language, academically gifted, and exceptional children departments as soon as the performance tasks were drafted so that differentiated tasks or instructional strategies could be written for each performance task. This was another first for the school district. The differentiated tasks and instructional strategies were specific Tier 1 activities and strategies for the classroom teacher to use that were aligned to the standards. While the teacher was still required to address the Individual Education Plans and 504 plans, these differentiation strategies helped the teacher adjust instruction for struggling and already proficient students. In addition to addressing all students' learning needs, this section of the unit was a vehicle for improving collaboration across departments. The curriculum was gaining the potential to be "viable and guaranteed" for every student.

The academically gifted department also began developing units for advanced ELA courses in middle school that are based on the units written for the general education setting. The math curriculum specialists developed units for the middle school advanced math courses. These units use more complex texts, include more advanced performance tasks, and, in some cases, compact the curriculum so that standards from the next grade are taught. These units are in addition to the differentiated strategies that are offered in the standard units.

Curriculum specialists worked diligently between Thanksgiving and the winter break to define, for each grade and subject, the instructional materials that are needed to support the new curriculum. The materials list was included in the 2012/13 budget request. Any unspent funds at the end of the 2010/11 fiscal year were used to purchase as many materials as possible so teachers would have instructional materials to begin the school year. Math specialists were fortunate and discovered a single resource that is well aligned to the Common Core standards and is available K–12.

The ELA team, on the other hand, identified specific ancillary texts that were needed to supplement instructional resources that were already in schools. For example, an ELA standard for second grade refers to comparing folktales from five different cultures. The current basal text contains only two folktales. Therefore, additional resources were identified to address this limitation. Additionally, the ELA team was concerned about appropriate text complexity in the current resources, so they also considered those elements when recommending supplemental texts.

A unit-writing rubric was developed to establish district common quality criteria for each component of the unit. As each unit was completed, the author was required to get specific feedback from a colleague for each component. The specialists valued the feedback from their peers since they knew that their peers were invested in maintaining the same level of quality. This quality control is also designed to assist the curriculum specialists as a tool for identifying teacher writers and as they vet each unit that teachers submit. The teacher leaders in grades 6–12 were given the rubric as a tool to revise their units as needed.

The January deadline came and went. The prioritized and "unwrapped" standards were ready to be posted, as were the clustered standards and pacing guides. Learning progressions had been completed as well. The first units, however, were not complete with peer review until April. An additional challenge was that the online curriculum management system, GEMS, was undergoing a revision. All materials were posted for leaders and teachers to see by June.

> *"I'm exhausted. I have learned so much, but these deadlines are killing me,"* said a math curriculum specialist.

Supporting Teachers

The district made a commitment to use all available surplus federal, state, and local funds to provide four days of lesson plan writing for the first math and ELA units of the 2012/13 school year at each grade, as well as to provide continued unit development during the summer. This was a formidable challenge in a district with approximately 5,000 classroom teachers. Teachers selected one of two weeks to attend for their grade and subject. A stipend was provided for each teacher who completed the four-day opportunity. Overall, the feedback was very positive and the teachers appreciated the level of rigor and detail in each unit. Teachers wrote and shared lesson plans with others across the district who teach the same subject and grade. Each elementary teacher selected math or ELA for the grade they will teach in the fall. The district is not requiring that the teachers use the new units. However, most principals will be looking for equal quality and rigor from those who choose not to use them.

In addition to the summer lesson writing, curriculum specialists worked with teacher writers during the summer of 2012 to continue working on unit development. The district goal is that *all* of the units for the first semester would be completed and posted on GEMS by the first day of school and that all of the units for the second semester be posted by the end of the first quarter. Teacher writers were paid to write these units, and they were provided with an exemplar unit from their subject and grade along with a unit rubric. Curriculum specialists provided the professional development and provided feedback as groups of teachers began writing additional units. As units are completed, the specialists will use the unit rubric to give feedback to writers and to vet the units before posting units to GEMS.

> *"It will be a challenge for teachers the first time they teach the unit because it's a new way of organizing what we want students to learn and how they will learn it," said an ELA classroom teacher.*

Where Are We Now?

By the first day of the 2012/13 school year, all first-quarter units were posted for teachers on GEMS in all subjects for Common Core and Essential State standards. More than 2,000 teachers attended lesson plan writing sessions during the summer and report that they are ready to implement the first unit. More than 20 teacher writers developed units during the summer. The curriculum specialists continued to review, revise, and post the remaining units for math and ELA. They will be challenged to meet the timeline and maintain the high quality of work. More than half of all of the units needed to teach the Common Core standards were written by August 2012. At that time, curriculum specialists continued to use the GCS vetting process before they were posted on GEMS.

> *"It was a pleasure to see our units begin coming to life during the summer lesson planning sessions. Some of the teachers will really struggle to teach these units but they were asking for more. They couldn't see themselves being able to write these units yet," said a curriculum specialist.*

What's Next?

The entire curriculum and instruction department has made a giant leap in providing teaching resources in a systematic and comprehensive model and in improving learning opportunities for all students. The units are designed to be dynamic, so over time the units will change and improve based on input from the teachers who use them. Each unit ends with an invitation for the teacher to provide feedback on the unit. After the unit is taught, teachers are asked: What worked well? What would you change? What were the challenges for the students? That feedback will be collected and reviewed by the curriculum specialists. Student achievement data from district-wide assessments will be reviewed and analyzed with respect to the units as well. Curriculum specialists will decide and prioritize the unit revisions as part of their work plan for 2012/13 and beyond.

The 2012/13 work will include continued unit development. Curriculum specialists will likely have far fewer teachers available to write the remaining units during the school year, so much of the work to complete and post additional units will rest with them.

Teachers have commented and worried about all of the new content in each subject. The curriculum specialists will need to develop teacher leaders to assist with the implementation of Common Core standards and collaborate with community colleges and universities to provide professional development in the content and instructional strategies for each discipline.

> *"I'm worried about all of the new content! We don't have the personnel to support the teachers," said a curriculum specialist.*

At the school, curriculum leaders will need to help teachers select particular units for implementation. Even an expert and accomplished teacher would be challenged to implement *all* of the new units, and the elementary teacher will be especially challenged to implement all units in all subjects every day. Professional learning communities will need to be at peak operation in order for teachers to share the work in understanding the new curriculum, interpreting assessments, responding to struggling and advanced students, and reflecting on the effectiveness of the new units. Smart schools will create a collaborative vision of the implementation of the new standards and units over the next three to five years so that staff has the stamina to "go for the long haul" in such a large undertaking. School leaders, including teacher leaders, will need to be aware of the stages of change and loss that will be apparent as teachers relinquish their tried and true to adopt the new.

At this point the teachers in Guilford County are expected, not required, to teach the first unit of the year with the newly written resources. All of the remaining units and corresponding professional development will be available to all teachers a semester prior to teaching them. Units will be revised and new ones added as long as the Common Core and Essential State standards are in place. Wouldn't it be fantastic if the fifth-grade teachers had a choice of many units that all addressed the cluster of standards that are taught during the first half of quarter 2? As teachers, schools, districts, and states collaborate, the possibilities are endless.

What Do the Teachers Say?

Rebecca McKnight, a grade 6 ELA teacher leader and unit writer, says:

> *"The process was a roller-coaster ride because we really didn't know what was expected in the very beginning. Previously our units were more topical than conceptual. We no longer have any novel studies in the sixth grade. We had to redefine what is meant by "text" and that has an impact on developing our units. Real-world assessments will take the place of quizzes and tests. That will be a real change!"*

A high school ELA teacher writer who piloted her unit with her students says:

> *"The exemplar unit allowed us to take what we thought would be a difficult standard and successfully teach it to a wide range of learners. Having the resources from the unit allowed me to work creatively with my students to make sure they were each able to complete the tasks at hand. The students enjoyed the engaging scenario, and they were able to branch out well beyond just writing about what they had learned. They were able to use visuals, technology, and their speaking skills, and create a product they were proud to share with other classes."*

Getting Started on Your Journey

As you reflect on Guilford County Schools' experience, think about how their story applies to you in your current setting, and then answer the following questions:

1. *Once the unit focus and primary concepts or skills were identified and the standards were clustered, the curriculum teams were able to develop pacing guides and write Big Ideas and the corresponding Essential Questions easily.*

   How does the process of creating pacing guides currently work in your school or district? Is your process effective? How do you know?

2. *For the first time, Guilford County Schools has specific scoring guides and rubrics that address all of the standards in math and ELA in every grade.*

   What does your current assessment model look like? Do you have a balance between formative and summative assessment, or are your assessments more weighted in one of the aforementioned categories? Do you have scoring guides to evaluate and monitor progress on the formative assessments you use?

3. *The entire curriculum and instruction department has made a giant leap in providing teaching resources in a systematic and comprehensive model and in improving learning opportunities for all students. The units are designed to be dynamic, so over time, the units will change and improve based on input from the teachers who use them. Each unit ends with an invitation for the teacher to provide feedback on the unit. After the unit is taught, teachers are asked: What worked well? What would you change? What were the challenges for the students? That feedback will be collected and reviewed by the curriculum specialists."*

   This account of how Guilford is going about unit writing, creation, and re-creation speaks to the notion that Rigorous Curriculum Design is a process, not a destination. Does this idea cause you doubt or relief? Explain.

CHAPTER NINE

West Haven Public Schools, West Haven, Connecticut

"The difference was noticeable to me immediately. After a brief presentation to the teams, the discourse began. After a while, our visitors, other school districts, and a college professor let us know that they were amazed at the quality of conversation they were hearing around the development of curriculum and its alignment to the Common Core State Standards. The conversations were rich and thoughtful. Teachers were automatically going through the Rigorous Curriculum Design process not only because they had experience with writing curriculum, but also because they understood its meaning. Further, they realize that if we continue on this path, we will be successful."

ANNE P. DRUZOLOWSKI

"Our curriculum is more focused. It is based on the CCSS, not on the published resources we have. It is integrated. It is meaningful. It allows for differentiated instruction. It encourages both student independence and collaborative work."

A WEST HAVEN LEADER

RCD District: West Haven Public Schools

Location: West Haven, Connecticut (Urban)

Population: 3,263 students

Author: Anne P. Druzolowski, Ph.D.,
Assistant Superintendent of Schools

Our journey to curriculum revision began in December 2008. From the very beginning, we urged all staff to improvise, revise, and communicate, saying: "Be willing to accept feedback from everyone. Do not be afraid to make any changes along the way. Do not wait until the end of the school year to modify anything." This sense of commitment and unity was reinforced as we brought all staff through the process of better understanding the tenets of curricula and the use of the Rigorous Curriculum Design model to establish that roadmap to successful student performance.

Demographic Description of West Haven Public Schools

West Haven is an urban district with a population of 55,564 located in southern Connecticut, adjacent to the large urban district of New Haven, along the coastline of the Long Island Sound. The population of the West Haven Public School System consists of 3,263 youngsters representing grades prekindergarten through grade 12. Staffing includes a total of 531 teachers, social workers and psychologists in every school, guidance counselors, special education teachers in all sites, and reading/mathematics specialists at all schools. There are six pre-K–4 elementary schools, one grades 5–6 elementary school, one grades 7–8 middle school, and one high school.

The West Haven community is composed of more than 60 cultures. The school system capitalizes on this diversity and celebrates multiculturalism in a variety of ways throughout the academic year. West Haven continues to build on the sense of community, which has been present for decades, and is best typified by the numerous family and community academic activities, as well as social and recreational activities, held at the schools. Events include international nights, school-wide research projects celebrating different cultures, family math nights, and other informational sessions and workshops, which are designed to involve all parents in their schools.

This brief description of West Haven provides depth to the process and practices we have embraced over the past four years. Without the caring and special staff that led this charge, we would not be committed to instructional changes as we are now. As a result of the staff's dedication, our story of change features success in the changes of adult behaviors that are as important and noticeable as the anticipated changes in student scores on state assessments.

Description of Our Initial RCD Journey

We are most proud of our efforts to implement a standards-based curriculum, which is complemented by the creation and use of common formative assessments. The curriculum review and implementation model is based on research from renowned educators, such as Larry Ainsworth and Dr. Douglas Reeves of The Leadership and Learning Center, and the Connecticut State Department of Education's Accountability for Learning Initiative (CALI), which they both assisted in developing. The efforts to improve student learning for all youngsters, regardless of their educational need or handicapping condition, is reflected in our newly revised curriculum, which is grounded in educational and scientific research, reflects state and national standards, differentiates instruction utilizing a variety of research-based strategies, and is consistently implemented across all schools and across all grade levels.

Why RCD?

We began our journey to build our curriculum "airplane" in January 2009 with systemic change in the entire education arena. West Haven's newly appointed superintendent, Neil Cavallaro, along with his newly appointed assistant superintendent (Anne P. Druzolowski, author of this chapter), clearly stated to the entire 500-plus members of the West Haven educational community: "This is a five-year plan. It is a process." This was the first movement toward educational reform in West Haven. Prior to this call for developing and implementing a holistic approach to change, little had been done within the district to systemically revise curricula, or to create a roadmap to system-wide improvement.

I had the opportunity to work with Larry Ainsworth in another Connecticut school district and understood the power of the Rigorous Curriculum Design model. The process provided our staff with a common philosophy and vocabulary for understanding the importance of curricula and the use of assessments and unit planning for instruction. We strongly believed, and still do, that all of our classroom teachers require a complete understanding of the RCD process, as well as the Connecticut Accountability for Learning Initiative, complemented by the district-wide professional development plan. This combination of endeavors was set to define our focus for instruction during the next five years.

Steps Taken to Implement Change (Begin the Airplane Flight)

West Haven's new administrators introduced to the board of education a five-year professional development action plan that the board subsequently adopted. This five-year plan incorporated all of the research-based components of the Connecticut Accountability for Learning Initiative:

1. Making standards work (prioritizing and "unwrapping" the K–12 state standards in all subject areas);

2. Common formative assessments;

3. Data-driven decision making;

4. Research-based instructional strategies;

5. School climate.

These core practices represent the heart of our changes, as displayed in a state-created graphic that we refer to as the "CALI flower" (Figure 9.1). While you do not see the term "Rigorous Curriculum Design" specifically mentioned within these four

FIGURE 9.1 The Connecticut Accountability for Learning Initiative (CALI)

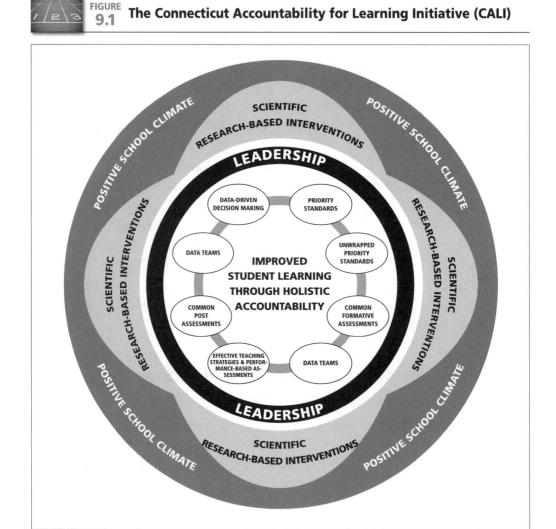

petals, it is important to realize that we operate from a holistic perspective within which RCD is embedded. We utilize RCD tenets within the "petals," such as the prioritizing and "unwrapping" of K–12 state standards, the planning of our units and pacing guides, and the development of common formative assessments. The data-driven decision making process, coupled with the use of research-based instructional strategies, provide our tools for improvement.

Making Standards Work

All staff members experienced the three-day Making Standards Work sessions, during which they learned the reasons why curriculum is powerful if done in a systemic fashion. Here, with guidance from Larry Ainsworth and The Leadership and Learning Center, our staff learned the importance of understanding and using the Rigorous Curriculum Design model. While *all* staff members, including school and central office administrators, were involved in the training, core teams of teachers were targeted to write the curricula to align with the state curriculum standards (prior to the introduction of the new Common Core State Standards). These teams were composed of grade-level teachers, English language learner teachers, and special education teachers. Teachers were split into two cohorts so as to facilitate the scheduling of work time for them to meet during the school day. The number of teachers in each cohort averaged about 120. District content-area supervisors were charged with the responsibility of overseeing the curricula work. All teachers were together in one space and were then able to examine the vertical alignment of the standards across grade levels.

The initial process of prioritizing the Connecticut state standards, "unwrapping" those standards, and developing corresponding units of study and pacing guides began immediately after completion of the Making Standards Work professional development series. The review of the existing curricula was done by our content-area supervisors. It is a recursive process coordinated between the district staff and the classroom teachers who are bringing the curricula to life every day.

Common Formative Assessment

Both cohorts received an introductory seminar about common formative assessments from Larry Ainsworth after prioritizing and "unwrapping" the standards and assigning them to grade- or course- specific units of study. CFAs and accompanying answer keys and scoring guides—directly aligned to the particular "unwrapped" Priority Standards—were developed. We accomplished our goal of having all cohort 1 (core content areas) curricular units of study with common formative assessments ready for lementation on the first day of school, September 2009. Production days began for cohort 2 (other content areas not considered core; e.g., visual and performing arts, P.E., technical education) in the fall of 2009. They were following cohort 1's model of unit development, but were a year behind.

Data-Driven Decision Making (DDDM) and Effective Teaching Strategies (ETS)

In order to better understand the importance of curriculum and its development and purpose, it was imperative that our district use the DDDM process as defined within the CALI flower. All schools used the data process to monitor instruction and make recommended changes to curricula, units of study, pacing, and common formative assessments as a result of analyzing data in teams. Embedded professional development and support to school teams, as well as to the district Data Team, was necessary, bringing successful and relevant meaning to the practice.

Concurrently, Effective Teaching Strategies seminars were offered through The Leadership and Learning Center, utilizing a two-stage approach. While attendance was not mandatory at that time, it would become so later on. Beginning in the spring of 2009, the high school special educators and the English language learner teachers were provided with a two-day ETS session from The Center. Our focus was on those staff members in need of immediate intervention relative to their teaching strategies. Since that time, we have offered five to six additional ETS sessions open to district staff on a first-come, first-served basis.

What We Learned from Our First Trip with Rigorous Curriculum Design

We learned so very much during our first two years of writing and implementing curriculum. Here are a few of our major take-aways:

1. Visibility of District Leaders and Common Language:

   • Leadership is imperative, but not sufficient. It must be *visible* from the assistant superintendent and central office leaders across to the school leaders. Attendance at Data Team meetings and all training sessions tells everyone about the importance of the initiative, as well as the message that *we are here with you* and *we believe in the process*. All of the central office staff has high visibility in the schools, thus enabling us to notice reoccurring themes relative to teacher, leadership, curriculum team writers', coaches' and facilitators', and central office professional development needs.

- Common vocabulary is the link to meaningful action. We learned a common language and we put that language within a context. It became meaningful and was communicated from the superintendent to the board members to the teachers and back again.

2. Teacher Ownership:

- Curriculum provided the staff with enough of a roadmap to allow for teacher creativity, and thus their craft, to shine through. Once teachers understood the importance of the roadmap, they felt comfortable knowing that they and others could connect the dots and allow the details to flow.

- First, however, they needed to understand the value of the curriculum and believe that they could identify tools and practices that would best support their teaching and learning of specific state/national standards.

- Curriculum did not necessarily mean prescriptive and scripted, but rather focused on providing guidance and support to all grade-level teachers, even if they taught in different buildings.

3. Collaboration Time:

- The importance of collaboration time cannot be overstated. We integrated scheduling collaboration time for all of our schools on a regular basis. District and school leaders heard teachers requesting time—not for planning independently, but rather with their content-area teams or grade-level teams during scheduled common planning time.

- Time was a necessary resource for the curriculum teams to practice the curriculum that they wrote, followed by the fleshing out of the units of study. During this time, as a team, they would make modifications and revisions to the way they would deliver and assess the curriculum.

- As time went on, the collaboration time was clearly defined as "Data Teams Time." All content-area teachers or grade-level teachers had the opportunity to meet, and to discuss successes and failures relative to the delivery of instruction. Agendas were shared in advance with principals and staff, and before long, Data Teams and professional learning communities became synonymous.

4. Instructional Materials and Resources:

• With a defined roadmap and unit planners, teachers requested specific resources to support their instruction. From the district level, anything they requested needed to "back into" the curriculum and be a long-term resource rather than a programmed kit or short-term fix.

• Assessment of available resources against a common curriculum, or in our case, identifying resources we lacked, was (and still is) necessary to make informed decisions. The district could examine the requests and determine what materials were required to complement and complete a common curriculum. We could also determine what professional development training and support was necessary to organize and implement from the district level.

5. Communication:

• Continually explaining to all administrators that it is necessary to have teachers out of the buildings more than usual for professional development and that support from administrators is "non-negotiable" is an ongoing task. If implementation is to be effective, this position must be supported by both the superintendent and the assistant superintendent.

• Using our administrative council meetings to get feedback from principals as to how the work was progressing and to keep them in the loop relative to curriculum changes and professional development planning.

• Making sure that principals conduct classroom visits on a regularly scheduled basis and that they speak honestly about problems and issues. It is mandatory, not optional, for the school leaders to be active participants in this process.

6. Organizing Professional Development Sessions and Production Days:

• Using part of the summer to plan professional development days and allocating additional days during the school year to continue developing units, all the while balancing the number of days that staff members are out of the buildings.

- Comfort, comfort, comfort! We did not skimp here. Acoustics needed to be good, copy machines available, resources plentiful, and lunches delicious. This is hard work, and we wanted to make conditions for *supporting* that work as pleasant as possible.

- Ordering early any resources required for production days and having them on hand for future use.

7. Passion for Teaching:

- Through the process, we relearned that we never stop growing. We question what we have written, how well it is communicated, and what more we need to provide our teaching staff to allow them to develop to their highest potential.

- The assistant superintendent's goal (*my* goal) was to reignite the passion for teaching—the primary reason most of our teachers *became* teachers. Although that sounds self-serving, I clearly wanted our staff to understand that curriculum was not a prescription for teaching, but rather a roadmap to clarify *what* we should be teaching, and then trusting them to decide how to deliver the content with passion and gusto.

We continued to revise curriculum and common formative assessments during the school year. This process was done primarily through our surveys and regular requests to provide us with feedback or questions about the units. The district coordinators then examined those results and determined if the assessments were as rigorous as they could be. This recursive practice remains critical to maintaining the visibility of the curriculum, instead of keeping it in a closet or on a classroom shelf.

After all of this work was accomplished, then came the Common Core!...

Common Core State Standards Integration (Building the Spaceship)

We were flying the state standards airplane and monitoring our flight plan as we went along when all of a sudden we were faced with a radical change in standards. Connecticut, like 45 other states, decided to adopt the Common Core State Standards to replace the *state* standards we had used to develop our curriculum. Interestingly, at the same time that this was happening, *Rigorous Curriculum Design* by Larry Ainsworth was published, and much about West Haven's work with RCD was included. (Author's note: Dr. Druzolowski's humility downplays the vital role West Haven played in developing the full breadth and depth of the RCD model—one of the many reasons *Rigorous Curriculum Design* is dedicated to the leaders and educators of West Haven, Connecticut.)

The CCSS are very rigorous and fast-paced standards. State standards that were previously taught at the upper grade levels were now found to appear in the lower grades. How would the state help districts better understand the volumes of new, much more rigorous Common Core standards in English language arts and mathematics? Would there be enough time to teach all of these new standards with equal emphasis?

The Connecticut State Department of Education asked Larry Ainsworth to assist in better understanding the CCSS and in preparing for changing curricula across the state. Because Larry had been very active in the development of the CALI model, his leadership in this field was well known. In January 2011, he met with approximately 100 math and English language arts experts from various school districts across Connecticut to prioritize and "unwrap" the Common Core standards within the context of the RCD model. Larry requested that our West Haven central office team (mathematics, science, language arts, and early childhood coordinators) support him in this effort, which we were happy to do.

Drawing from our experience in prioritizing the Connecticut standards, we were able to support the state design teams as they worked through the prioritization of the Common Core. We were able to share with our state colleagues what we had learned about the RCD process and its value. We concluded the nine days with good information about a model of curriculum redesign directly aligned to the CCSS. The state eventually decided that they would not create a common state curriculum, but rather would disseminate the Common Core State Standards we had prioritized within the five foundational steps of the RCD framework as a suggested beginning for writing local curriculum.

Next Steps

It was now apparent that we would need to begin the process yet again at the *district* level. However, we had several factors in our favor:

- We knew the RCD process "cold," as we had been using the RCD model curriculum for over two years;
- We had been *revising* the curriculum on a continual basis to make it more clear, more precise, and more rigorous;
- We had a common vocabulary;

- We had the same leadership in place at the schools and at the district level;

- We had moved into performance-based tasks, with Larry Ainsworth leading a cohort of curriculum writers at the high school;.

- Collaboration time was in place, scheduled, and getting better every day;

- We all believed in the process.

The only concern I had was that I was not sure how teachers and administrators would feel about another round of curriculum writing this soon. However, we were pleasantly surprised.

The advantage of being "fresh off" curriculum writing using the RCD model was that we knew how to organize for the rewrites. Larry was still involved in our district as we worked on other related issues, so we took advantage of this opportunity to begin our revision work during the 2011/12 school year, using many of the same steps we had first used in 2009–2011:

Step 1: Gathering information on the CCSS at the central office level. Connecticut is a governing state for the Smarter Balanced Assessment Consortium, so we visited the SBAC Web site regularly to keep ourselves informed. In addition, the mathematics and language arts district coordinators, accompanied by our science, ELL, and early childhood coordinator and special education staff, attended many events that highlighted the CCSS, such as dinner meetings with professional organizations, state workshops on the CCSS, and regional meetings for coordinators.

Step 2: Starting the CCSS buzz across the school system. Everywhere we went, we introduced the terminology of the Common Core and let everyone know that changes were being made on a national level. We informed the board of education that this was a repeat performance of curriculum writing and assessment. "Rigor and depth of knowledge" became a phrase we casually dropped into every conversation. We knew the importance of communicating, so we shared SBAC links with teachers, administrators, and the community.

Step 3: Training sessions for mathematics coaches and reading/language arts consultants were imperative. These staff would be our coordinators' support as we began the rewrites. They needed to begin some of the process so we could determine what we were up against relative to professional development and other resource needs. These individuals would present in May 2012 to grade-level groups of teachers at their assigned schools the basics of the CCSS and our next push to revise and align the curriculum accordingly.

Step 4: Review of current resources to determine potential conflicts with the new standards. We finally decided to purchase a new resource in mathematics to support the curriculum and our unit plans. Fortunately, review of these materials in light of the CCSS indicated that we needed to cross-reference to a textbook/resource review that was overdue by 10 years We ultimately made the decision not to move ahead with any purchase, deciding instead to wait until we feel the products clearly support the CCSS. Meanwhile, we have purchased multiple resources to support our reading intervention plan.

Step 5: Curriculum writers were selected for mathematics and reading/language arts. These individuals were largely drawn from those teachers who had written curriculum two years prior and were using the curriculum with much success. Some changes in assignments had to be made as writers had been assigned to different grade levels. We utilized the same process as in the past: PK–12 grade-level groups for mathematics and English language arts, with four or five teachers per group. Department heads, coaches, and reading consultants were on hand to support specific grade levels or content areas, as they were well versed in the CCSS. Special education staff was represented on the teams.

Step 6: Begin the writing. In April 2012, we began our first four days with Larry Ainsworth, who reviewed our units and supported all of us as we began the rewrite process. Over 100 staff members were in the same professional development facility as we had been before, and they were focused, excited, and producing. The old, "oh not again" attitude never surfaced as our teacher leaders dug in and got to know the new standards. Individuals and organizations who knew of our efforts came to observe the RCD process and were very impressed with the involvement of all staff.

Step 7: Easy Does It, But Hurry! If I learned one thing during my last curriculum writing project, it was to ask the teachers how much they felt they could accomplish for the September 2012 start date of new unit implementation. They realized that we could not possibly finish all units for September; however, they could finish the first *half* of the year's units. The Central Office Team made the decision that, minimally, *all teachers* needed to have the opportunity to review and question the curriculum changes, the common formative assessments, and the authentic performance tasks prior to September. It was decided that no later than the first week in July, units and assessments for the first half of the school year would be available to teachers on our Web site. In English language arts, the curriculum writers recognized and voiced the need for more time to complete the major changes their units required.

Step 8: Two days of production time were set for May. Larry Ainsworth provided our staff with training in understanding the power and use of authentic performance tasks. We agreed that initially we would include only one performance task per unit.

Step 9: Utilizing an "accordion approach" for review of units as they were finished. Teachers were e-mailed the draft units and had the opportunity to ask for clarification, provide feedback if they did not particularly agree with the Big Ideas or Essential Questions, or to make any other recommendations for revision. Those ideas were then reviewed by the curriculum writers, who either incorporated the changes or did not. The assistant superintendent spot-checked units for quality and rigor. Final reviews of all curricula and assessments were made by the coordinators and key curriculum coaches and consultants.

Step 10: Final production days. The final production time for all teams was set for the last week in June 2012. Staff was provided a stipend for the completion of the curriculum, as agreed upon prior to the writing. Curriculum writers did not meet in one location for this writing; now that school was out, they could meet wherever they were comfortable. District coordinators would visit their writing sites, address questions, and review pieces of curriculum. We wanted to ensure that they would continue to receive support throughout this process.

Step 11: District coordinator final review. Upon completion of each grade-level/content-area unit, the unit and assessment was submitted to the district coordinator for a final review and edit. Following this was a final return to the teams for any further rewrites. When the units were completed, they were placed on our Web site for teacher review over the summer. All curricula are considered "drafts"—works in progress visible to all. We find that by giving this status to our curriculum, teachers are receptive to suggestions and feedback and always want to improve their products.

Step 12: Resource review and professional development. We are in the process of examining the prioritized resource lists submitted by design teams and determining what we should purchase to support instruction. Part of the review includes not only alignment of instructional resources and materials to the

CCSS, but also the professional development support necessary for teachers to develop their expertise in delivery of the CCSS-based units of study.

Step 13: Second half of the year writing. Writing teams will be meeting during the months of September through December 2012 in order to finish the remaining units. We will be relying on any and all new information from SBAC to determine what other changes we will need to make.

Step 14: Performance tasks and assessments. Performance tasks and assessments are very powerful tools to deliver instruction. No longer are teachers the "sage on stage," as Larry likes to say, but rather the facilitator of learning—the "guide on the side." We will provide much professional support through classroom modeling during the school year, as well as explicit instruction wherever needed or requested.

Clearly, we believe that the RCD process of writing curriculum and the development of aligned assessments has tapped teacher potential and rekindled in all the passion for teaching.

Professional Development for Staff

Professional development, regardless of the curriculum model or initiative offered, must be in place to guide any big-picture design. It is not sufficient to have professional development for the sake of having professional development. With the advent of the CCSS, we identified several areas of needed professional development for teachers that they will be required to attend next year. Professional development includes both embedded support within classrooms or in schools, and support outside the school environment. The following are a few of the key areas we are targeting for professional development during the next five years.

- *Understanding/clarifying how performance-based tasks improve learning for youngsters, as well as how they effect change in teaching styles.* Performance-based tasks, as teaching tools, become resources for our teachers that bring learning to life, make it relevant, and make students think. To better understand their impact, it is imperative that classroom teachers use more performance-based tasks and examine adult behavior changes combined with student outcome data within their Data Teams.

- *Better understanding of rigor.* We need to define and practice rigor rather than assume it is "more of the same" and not a deeper understanding of a standard or topic. The extension of thinking skills plays a huge role for both the teacher and the student.

• *Supporting teachers as they practice instructional strategies within the classroom.* We have provided numerous instructional strategies to our teachers, both in a conventional professional development format as well as within Data Teams. We will be moving to embed more of this training within the classrooms via our literacy coaches in mathematics and in English language arts. Using modeling and coaching support to emphasize not only the appropriate use of a particular strategy, but also the fidelity with which it is operationalized, is critical for a successful outcome.

• *English language learners and special education children require strategies that support them as they access the content, whatever that may be.* To that end, we have enhanced our unit plans to include more of these strategies for all teachers. We will continue providing both embedded professional development and group professional development that targets strategy development and enactment for our teachers.

• *Monitoring the use of RCD within the classroom is training that our administrators need to have.* While they have been involved in all aspects of implementing our CALI model, leaders need to move to the next level. The leadership academy for all of our administrators will focus on defining what we should be seeing consistently in the classroom, how to better understand the purpose and quality of the unit planner, and how to best support change in adult behaviors.

Positive Changes

There were so many positive changes the first time around with the RCD process. Most of the changes were in the form of teachers' reactions to new information and the manner in which they produced curriculum. Attention was focused on translating the process Larry Ainsworth presented into a *product*; there was initial uncertainty about how that product would be received by the district teachers. The second time, however, provided me with a new appreciation of the RCD process. It *has* changed adult behaviors and brought conversations to a new and higher professional level.

There were many, many passionate professional conversations. By now, all 100 West Haven curriculum writers/teachers and coordinators are very familiar with the RCD process and have enjoyed working with their teams. This difference was noticeable to me immediately. After a brief presentation to the teams, the discourse began. After a while, our visitors, other school districts, and a college professor let us know that they were amazed at the quality of conversation they were hearing around the development of curriculum and its alignment to the CCSS. The conversations were rich and thoughtful. Teachers were automatically going through the Rigorous Curriculum Design process not only because they had experience with writing curriculum, but also because they understood its meaning. Further, they realized that if we continue on this path, we will be successful.

West Haven teachers are the ultimate professionals. Their conversations are rich and exciting. Their discourse is about their craft. When staff members go out for interviews, or are with their peers from other districts, they let me know that they feel confident and knowledgeable about teaching and learning. They are the best! To say the least, I felt like a proud mama watching the passion continue to grow.

The behaviors of children are difficult enough to change, let alone that of adults. I could envision someone saying … "Oh no! Not this again." But there was not a word of that. Adult behavior has changed during the past two years. *All conversations are professional and challenging and collegial.* I firmly believe that adult behaviors can change if those adults see value in the outcome. Clearly, RCD has provided that for our teachers and enabled us to continue moving ahead.

The units that we are now reviewing are much more rigorous than what we had developed two years ago. Some of that is because the CCSS are more rigorous. While we still have much to do in the area of perfecting the depth with which we teach a standard, we are farther ahead than we were two years ago. Our coordinators have been reviewing the curricular units and assessments and see that while we may still have progress to make, we are on the right track and we have a much better understanding of the concept of *rigor*. We were not at this juncture two years ago.

Most importantly, teachers are beginning to see the relationship of performance-based tasks to teaching and its dramatic impact on student learning. It has been powerful to create a curriculum that provides activities that go beyond a book report or a culminating project. We are beginning to become more experienced in the writing of performance-based tasks, while wanting to become even better.

Future Needs and Plans

Any curriculum writing process involves continual use and review of the content, coordinating of assessments, and the need for rewrites. The word "draft" on our curriculum indicates that it is just that—a continual working *draft* that we are making better every year through practice and use. Using the "accordion process" to write-review-edit-review-review-edit-print (Figure 9.2) has meant that all staff has a role and an opportunity to provide feedback to this living curriculum.

Our plan is to continue using this review process while we write the remaining half of the curriculum from September through December 2012. This process encourages ownership of the curriculum development process by the teachers as a direct result of their input. We will continue to incorporate staff suggestions for revision into our units, document staff development needs, and plan for further revisions of units during the spring of 2013.

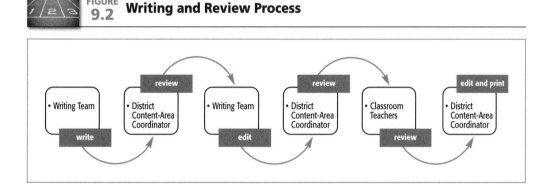

FIGURE 9.2 Writing and Review Process

Progress monitoring of student growth depends on two primary factors: (1) a strong curriculum and (2) the fidelity and consistency with which the curriculum is implemented within the classroom to guide instruction. The review of curriculum and the resulting edits only make a curriculum stronger from the perspective of teacher ownership, as well as increasing the content depth and the rigor defined within the curriculum. *How* the curriculum is consistently used within the classroom is what brings about student growth.

As we continue to monitor effective delivery of the curriculum, resulting student growth indicators, and adult behavior changes, our challenge will be to remain patient and to give staff the necessary support.

Keeping the door open for revisions during the course of the school year while the curriculum is being used is critical to making immediate changes or changes to be incorporated the following school year. While teachers do provide input on a regular basis, our district coordinators will formally solicit responses from the teachers via a survey conducted twice per year. Through this venue, we will document staff suggestions relative to curriculum clarification or revisions throughout the school year for curriculum teams to review and reflect in their editing of units. During the late spring of 2013, we will be revising our curriculum in mathematics and English language arts. We are also looking at beginning the same process of curriculum review and alignment to the new Next Generation science standards. Science curriculum writing teams used the RCD process two years ago with much success. They will be our cohort 2.

Survey Results from Curriculum Writing Teams

During the revising of our curriculum to align with the CCSS, we asked several questions on a short professional development survey to inform us of the leadership development the RCD process has provided our 100 curriculum writers. The survey, while not perfect, did give us some insight as to what we need to do to support our developing teacher leaders. The following provides a glimpse into what the survey indicated we need to work on.

With regard to the professional nature of writing curriculum and its effect on instruction, our 100 curriculum writers (teachers) indicated that they are now instructing much better; in fact:

- 91 percent indicated that the development and use of performance-based assessments will improve teacher instruction;

- 98 percent of the teachers utilize instructional strategies based on student need;

- 86 percent select instructional strategies that align to the content in the unit;

- 82 percent use pretest data to inform instruction;

- 88 percent of writers contribute to a Data Team on a regular basis.

From the leadership perspective:

- 80 percent of the teachers felt that writing curriculum and formative assessments has positively affected interaction with peers;

- 91 percent of the surveyed staff felt that performance-based assessments will definitely change the way they teach;

- 74 percent of curriculum writers believe they are sought out because of their working knowledge of the construction of assessments;

- 68 percent of curriculum writers believe they are a resource to teachers relative to the interpretation of curriculum;

- 50 percent still feel that they are not perceived as leaders in the building.

Other data reinforce the idea that curriculum writers do not perceive themselves as being the instructional leaders in the buildings. This information, while not conclusive, provides us with some direction as to what we need to do to support teacher leadership within the schools.

Survey Insights About *Prospective* West Haven Teachers

One question on the survey that provided us with much insight as to our curriculum writers' belief system about the recursive curriculum writing process was this: "What information about our changes in teaching and learning would you provide new teachers who want to work in West Haven?"

What follows is a representative sampling of the responses and recurring themes that emerged within them. It is these comments that show the high degree of professionalism and dedication West Haven teachers and leaders display and why. I have the greatest admiration and respect for them.

What information about our changes in teaching and learning would you provide new teachers who want to work in West Haven?

- "The changes in teaching and learning are those that reflect changes in our world and our students. All teachers, especially those who would like to work in West Haven, should believe in and support the revolutionary ideas and changes underway in our district, and be prepared to work hard in order to fully implement them."

> *"West Haven has a strong professional development program and support from administration to implement changes. It is a hands-on, 'buckle down' atmosphere, striving for improvement."*

- "Teachers must be learners themselves."

- "Our curriculum is more focused. It is based on the CCSS, not on the published resources we have. It is integrated. It is meaningful. It allows for differentiated instruction. It encourages both student independence and collaborative work."

- "I would inform any new teacher who wants to work in West Haven that we have become a proactive school district rather than reactive. We have created a strong framework in which our teachers are an important part."

- "[West Haven] curriculum is rigorous—prepare to have high standards: less whole-group instruction and more small groups (differentiated instruction), and know that data drives [our] instruction."

- "Change is good! It opens up new ideas that focus on results. You are not working harder, but smarter, and seeing results in the classroom. Not only will students feel good, you will feel good as well."

- "We start with an *end* in mind. We think 'backwards,' and this helps to guide our instruction. Pretest data, if used right, is very powerful. It drives instruction; less is more—it is a laser-like focus on skills that need reteaching, etc."

- "It [curriculum] is going to be a *rigorous* curriculum. It is a work in progress and each school will deliver curriculum based on students' needs."

- "Teachers have a lot of input into the curriculum."

- "We are committed to changing the ways in which we view our profession."

- "West Haven continues to persevere in staff development."

- "Rigor is more important than covering many topics."

- "Performance-based assessments will help teachers teach according to student needs and become much more specific in their instruction."

"A new teacher in West Haven would need to understand that instruction is data-driven, that we are working toward providing rigorous instruction to all levels of students. Instruction should meet the needs of all students."

Getting Started on Your Journey

As you reflect on West Haven Public Schools' account, think about how their story applies to you in your current setting, and then answer the following questions:

1. *We need to define and practice rigor rather than assume it is "more of the same" and not a deeper understanding of a subject or topic. The extension of thinking skills plays a huge role for both the teacher and the student.*

    With the Common Core State Standards come increased levels of rigor and complexity. What does the word *rigor* mean to you? What can you do to increase the levels of rigor when it comes to instruction in your classroom, school, or district?

2. *The behaviors of children are difficult enough to change, never mind asking adults to change their behaviors. All I could envision was someone saying, "Oh no! Not this again." But there was not a word of that. Adult behavior had changed during the past two years. All conversations are professional and challenging and collegial. No one complained that they had to write yet another curriculum using different standards in such a short window of time. I firmly believe that adult behaviors can change if those adults see value in the outcome. Clearly, RCD provided that for our teachers and enabled us to continue moving ahead.*

    Reflect upon an experience in your setting where you have seen a change in adult practices and actions. Do you believe adult behaviors can change if the adults see value in the outcome as this author does? If so, when have you experienced this firsthand? If not, what do you believe motivates adults to change?

3. *Any curriculum writing process involves continual use and review of the content, coordinating of assessments, and rewrites. The word "draft" plastered on our curriculum indicates that it is just that—a continual working draft that we are making better every year through practice and use.*

West Haven's approach to curriculum design allows for continuous rewrites, edits, and changes by the teachers/designers themselves. This is unique to many other approaches that involve a one-time committee, or a commercial program purchase with a few days of training. How does your school or district approach curriculum design? Have you purchased your curriculum? Did you assemble a committee to write your curriculum and then distribute it to everyone? Or is your curriculum comprised of living, breathing documents that allow for continuous revision and refinement to address the needs of students as units are taught? Explain.

Conclusion

The majority of school systems in the United States are now, for the first time in our nation's history, all on the same journey to implement common national standards and prepare for common national assessments. The districts that have so generously contributed their time, thought, and energy to share within these pages the story of their "RCD journey so far" will see their influence extending far beyond the borders of their own school districts. All of us at The Leadership and Learning Center offer our sincere thanks to each and every one of you for sharing your story of implementation that is sure to benefit so many others.

For those of you who haven't begun planning curricular units based on the Common Core, or haven't quite settled on the steps you will take, remember, every worthwhile journey begins with a single course of action. In the words of Mark Twain, "The secret of getting ahead is getting started. The secret of getting started is breaking your complex, overwhelming tasks into small manageable tasks, and then starting on the first one." It is our hope that the accounts in this book have given you some practical ideas on how to break down what seems like an enormous task into one that is not just manageable, but rewarding and that results in dramatic increases in student achievement.

Those who have started the CCSS curriculum design journey should please keep in mind, and remind one another, especially when the challenges of daily life press in upon you, that this sometimes overwhelming work of revamping your curricula is a "process, and not an event—a marathon, and not a sprint." The common goal that unites us all is our commitment to work together for the good of each and every one of the students within our care and sphere of influence.

Whether you are new to the RCD process or already well underway, we invite you to share your ongoing story of implementation with us. Know that at any time we are here to serve and assist you in any way that we can.

With sincerest thanks for all you do for education and for the students you serve,

—Larry Ainsworth and Kristin Anderson

RCD Overview

This is an overview of parts two and three of the Rigorous Curriculum Design model: building a strong curricular foundation and designing the curricular units of study, respectively. Part four of the model explains how to implement each unit of study. Each step is described in detail with examples in its corresponding chapter of *Rigorous Curriculum Design* (Ainsworth, 2010).

Build a Strong Curricular Foundation (5 Steps)

Before constructing the curricular units of study, it is necessary to first build a strong foundation. Otherwise, curriculum design teams are erecting a superstructure upon an uncertain base. Here is a brief description of each of the five foundational steps:

1. **Prioritize the Standards.** Prioritize and vertically align from grade to grade and course to course the academic content standards (grade- or course-specific CCSS and state standards) for selected content areas. These represent the "assured competencies" that students are to know and be able to do by the end of each academic school year so they are prepared to enter the *next* level of learning.

2. **Name the Units of Study.** Name all of the specific units of study for each grade level and course in those selected content areas. Through these units of study, implemented during the year or course, students will learn and be assessed upon their understanding and application of the particular standards in focus.

3. **Assign Priority Standards and Supporting Standards.** Assign Priority Standards *and* supporting standards to each unit of study, taking into account "learning progressions"—those building blocks of concepts and skills that students need to learn before they can learn other ones. Confirm that every Priority Standard is assigned to more than one unit of study. Take care not to "overload" any one unit with too many standards, especially supporting standards.

4. **Prepare a Pacing Calendar.** Referring to the school district master calendar, create a curriculum pacing calendar for implementing the

units of study to ensure that all Priority Standards will be taught, assessed, retaught, and reassessed throughout the entire school year. Factor in a "buffer" week *between* units for the purpose of re-teaching and reassessing close-to-proficient students, intervening and reassessing far-from-proficient students, and enriching proficient and above students. Decide which units will be implemented before and after state/national exams. Adjust the length and/or duration of each unit of study so that all units can be effectively implemented before the end of the school year.

5. **Construct the Unit Planning Organizer.** Brainstorm a list of elements to include on a unit planning organizer that will be used to create each unit of study. Draft a sample template that includes all of these elements. Revise the template as needed while designing the curricular units.

Design the Curricular Units, from Start to Finish (12 Steps)

With the standards foundation in place, design each curricular unit of study, from start to finish. Here is a synopsis of each of the 12 sequential steps for doing so. Be sure all of these elements (except the weekly and daily planners) appear in the agreed-upon unit planning organizer.

1. **"Unwrap" the Unit Priority Standards.** "Unwrap" the assigned Priority Standards for *each specific unit of study* to determine the specific, teachable concepts and skills (what students need to know and be able to do) within those standards.

2. **Create a Graphic Organizer.** Create a graphic organizer (outline, bulleted list, concept map, or chart) as a visual display of the "unwrapped" concepts and skills, organized into three sections: one that lists the teachable concepts, one that lists each skill with its related concept(s), and one that shows the *approximate* levels of Bloom's Taxonomy and Webb's Depth of Knowledge for each concept-skill pair. Matching each skill and related concept(s) with the thinking skill levels reveals the skill's degree of *rigor*.

3. **Decide the Big Ideas and Essential Questions.** Decide the topical Big Ideas (foundational understandings, student "aha's") derived from the "unwrapped" concepts and skills for that unit of study. Write Essential Questions that will engage students to discover for

themselves the related Big Ideas and state them in their own words by the end of the unit.

4. **Create the End-of-Unit Assessment.** Create the end-of-unit assessment (either individual classroom or common formative *post-*assessment) directly aligned to the "unwrapped" Priority Standards and their levels of rigor. Include a blend of multiple-choice, short constructed-response, and extended constructed-response questions. Align the concepts, skills, and format of the end-of-unit assessment with district benchmark assessments (K–8) or midterms and finals/end-of-course exams (9–12). Reference SBAC or PARCC sample assessment items to ensure that end-of-unit assessment questions reflect the same rigor, formats, and vocabulary of these items.

5. **Create the Unit Pre-Assessment.** Create the pre-assessment aligned or "mirrored" to the post-assessment. "Aligned" means the questions are directly matched to those on the post-assessment but may be fewer in number. "Mirrored" means the pre-assessment will include the exact number and type of questions that will appear on the post-assessment.

6. **Identify Additional Vocabulary Terms, Interdisciplinary Connections, and 21st-Century Learning Skills.** In addition to the vocabulary of the "unwrapped" Priority Standards concepts, identify other specific academic or technical vocabulary from the supporting standards and text materials that students will need to learn during the unit. Identify any interdisciplinary connections and 21st-century learning skills to emphasize when planning engaging learning experiences and related instruction.

7. **Plan Engaging Learning Experiences.** Design meaningful learning activities directly based upon the "unwrapped" concepts and skills, additional vocabulary terms, interdisciplinary connections, and 21st-century learning skills. Plan engaging learning experiences— authentic performance tasks with real-world applications—that challenge students to utilize deep thought, investigation, and communication. Create accompanying scoring guides (rubrics) as the means for obtaining objective evidence of student learning relative to the standards in focus. Confirm that the planned learning experiences will give students the conceptual and procedural

understanding of the "unwrapped" concepts and skills represented on the end-of-unit post-assessment *and* "deliver" students to the Big Ideas of the unit.

8. **Gather Resource Materials.** Gather print materials and seek out technology resources that support the planned learning experiences for the unit. Select the most appropriate instructional resources and materials available that will assist students in learning and applying the "unwrapped" concepts and skills and discovering the Big Ideas.

9. **Select High-Impact Instructional Strategies.** Select high-impact instructional strategies (research-based, differentiation, enrichment, intervention, special education, English language learner) to use during instruction and related learning activities with the whole class, with small groups, and with individual students that have specific learning needs.

10. **Detail the Unit Planning Organizer.** Determine what additional details are needed to supplement the generally worded information on the unit planning organizer. For example: an instructional pacing and sequence of the "unwrapped" concepts and skills based on "learning progressions" (the sequence of concepts and skills students need to know and be able to do as prerequisites for learning the next set of concepts and skills); a listing of key teaching points, and suggested instructional strategies for specific students based on their learning needs (advanced students, at-risk students, special education students, English language learners) that teachers can reference when planning differentiated lessons and unit activities.

11. **Create Informal Progress-Monitoring Checks.** Find, design, or suggest quick, informal checks for student understanding (exit slips, short-answer questions, thumbs up/down, etc.)—*aligned to the end-of-unit assessment and administered in conjunction with "learning progressions"*—for educators to use during the unit of study in order to gauge student understanding and adjust instruction accordingly.

12. **Write the Weekly Plan; Design the Daily Lessons.**** Write the weekly lesson plan to implement the unit of study in weekly "installments," using it to guide and focus instruction of the targeted "unwrapped" concepts and skills and engage students in the planned learning experiences and assessments. Design the daily lessons to

align with the related weekly plan. (**Note: These are the tasks of classroom teachers, not the curriculum designers, although curriculum design teams can create weekly and daily blank planners that align with the other RCD planners.)

How to Implement Each Unit of Study (14 Steps)

When the unit planning organizers are completed and ready to use, implement each of the units according to the scheduled pacing calendars. Here is a brief description of the 14 steps for doing so:

1. **Introduce the Unit of Study to Students.** Present the unit's Essential Questions to students and explain that they will be able to respond to these questions in their own words by the end of the unit. Preview for students the "unwrapped" concepts and other academic vocabulary terms they will be learning and applying.

2. **Administer the Unit Pre-Assessment.** Set the stage by first explaining to students the purpose of a pre-assessment (not for a grade, but to find out what they already know and don't know about the upcoming unit of study so that the teacher can plan instruction accordingly). Then administer the common formative pre-assessment (or individual classroom pre-assessment, if not part of a collaborative team).

3. **Score and Analyze Student Data.** Score and analyze student pre-assessments individually or with colleagues in grade-level or course-specific instructional Data Teams to diagnose student learning needs.

4. **Decide How to Differentiate Instruction.** Referring to the unit details provided with the unit planning organizer, decide how to differentiate instruction for specific students based on assessment evidence—including the enrichment of any students who are already proficient prior to unit instruction.

5. **Begin Teaching the Unit.** Begin teaching the planned unit of study, flexibly grouping students according to their learning needs and using identified instructional strategies.

6. **Administer Progress-Monitoring Checks.** Administer frequent, informal progress-monitoring checks aligned to the end-of-unit

assessment—that coincide with the building-block progression of "unwrapped" concepts and skills—in order to make accurate inferences regarding students' understanding. These informal checks will assist individual educators and instructional Data Teams in monitoring the effectiveness of their targeted teaching strategies for the unit.

7. **Differentiate Instruction Based on Progress-Monitoring Checks.** Modify and adjust instruction for individual students, small groups, and/or the entire class based on the results of the informal checks for understanding.

8. **Schedule Mid-Unit Evaluation of Instructional Strategies.** Schedule a mid-unit evaluation of the targeted teaching and differentiation strategies to determine their effectiveness. During this meeting, participating teachers will share effective use of the targeted strategies and may decide to change any strategies that are not accomplishing their intended purpose. Individual educators who are not part of an instructional Data Team will reflect on the effectiveness of their own selected strategies and make any needed changes.

9. **Continue Teaching the Unit.** During the remaining weeks of the unit, continue teaching the "unwrapped" concepts and skills in the predetermined "learning progressions" sequence for specific learning activities and engaging learning experiences (authentic performance tasks). Continue using the targeted instructional strategies with all students, different groups of students, and individual students as planned.

10. **Continue Modifying and Adjusting Instruction.** Continue modifying and adjusting instruction as needed for individual students, small groups, and/or the entire class based on evidence derived from ongoing progress-monitoring checks.

11. **Administer End-of-Unit Assessment.** Administer the common formative post-assessment (or individual end-of-unit assessment if not part of a collaborative team).

12. **Score and Analyze Student Data.** Score and analyze student data individually or with colleagues in grade-level or course-specific instructional Data Teams. Celebrate successes! Plan how to address students' identified learning needs during the "buffer" week.

13. **Enrich, Remediate, and Intervene.** During a "buffer" week scheduled between the unit of study just completed and the next one scheduled, reteach *differently* those students who are still not proficient; use Tier 2 and 3 intervention strategies and other appropriate strategies for at-risk students. Reassess all non-proficient students. Enrich those students who are proficient and advanced.

14. **Reflect and Begin Again.** When the unit is officially completed, reflect individually and/or with colleagues about what worked well and what, if anything, should be changed the next time the unit is implemented. Take a deep breath, redirect your focus, and then repeat the process with the next unit of study.

RCD Unit Development Guide 1.0

As stated in the Introduction, we recognize the need for an objective set of guiding criteria to evaluate the *quality* of RCD units of study. To meet this need, we present here the Rigorous Curriculum Design Unit Development Guide 1.0. This tool is one that designers can reference as they initially create the units and/or later use to critique their completed first-draft unit products. Referencing the section-by-section specific criteria—descriptors of needed elements and quality related to each of the steps in the RCD model—design teams can identify where they need to make revisions to their initial unit drafts. Simply check the criteria that are evident in the unit drafts, and highlight those criteria in need of revision. Offer related suggestions or comments for a specific section in the adjacent space provided. Curriculum supervisors can utilize the RCD Unit Development Guide when conducting peer reviews of units that have been submitted for feedback. District design teams may also wish to include criteria for additional sections of their unit planning organizer that are specific to their own school district (e.g., Universal Lesson Design, key teaching points, etc.).

Rigorous Curriculum Design
Unit Development Guide 1.0

The following criteria are provided for use when designing or reviewing RCD units of study. Please check off each essential element that is included and complete. Provide any comments or feedback that will enable the unit designer to make any necessary adjustments or revisions.

Grade Level, Subject, and Name of Unit: _____

Reviewer(s): _____

Unit Identifying Information		
	Essential Element	**Comment(s) / Feedback**
	Includes Identifying Unit Information (i.e., Subject, Grade/Course, Name of Unit)	
	Indicates Type of Unit (Topical, Skills-Based, or Thematic/ Interdisciplinary)	
	Pacing Includes Number of Instruction Days and Number of "Buffer" Days (for Remediation and Enrichment)	

Unit Standards—Overarching, Priority, Supporting, Interdisciplinary

	Essential Element	Comment(s) / Feedback
	Lists Overarching Standards (Those Emphasized in All Units)	
	Lists **Bolded**, Full Text and Coding of Targeted <u>Priority</u> Standards for Unit	
	Lists Full Text and Coding of <u>Supporting</u> Standards for Unit	
	Lists Full Text and Coding of <u>Interdisciplinary</u> Standards	
	Limits Total Number of Unit Standards to Ensure Depth of Instruction and Student Understanding	

"Unwrapped" Priority Standards ONLY

	Essential Element	Comment(s) / Feedback
	<u>Underlines</u> Teachable Concepts (Nouns, Noun Phrases) and CAPITALIZES Skills (Verbs) Students Are to Know/Do	
	Connects Skills to Concepts on Graphic Organizer with Parenthetical Side-by-Side Notation, e.g., • DETERMINE (main idea) • CONVERT (fraction to decimal)	
	Identifies Approximate Levels of Bloom's (1-6) and Depth of Knowledge (1-4) for Each Skill	
	Graphic Organizer Represents *All* "Unwrapped" Concepts and Skills from Priority Standards ONLY	

Essential Questions

	Essential Element	Comment(s) / Feedback
	Represent Learning Goals for Unit of Study	
	Reflect *Content* and *Rigor* of "Unwrapped" Priority Standards	
	Include Higher-Level Questions, e.g., • Why do authors use literary devices? • When and how do we use estimation in daily life?	
	Are Written in Student-Friendly Language	
	Require Thought, Discussion, Investigation to Answer	
	Lead Students to Their Own Discovery of Big Ideas	

Big Ideas

	Essential Element	Comment(s) / Feedback
	Represent Desired Student Responses to Teacher's Essential Questions	
	Written Succinctly in Complete Statements (3 to 4 Maximum)	
	Reflect Explicit and/or Inferential Connections Students Are to Make and Retain After Instruction Concludes	
	Convey Value or Long-Term Benefit of Learning to Students	
	Topical Statements (Specific to Priority Standards in Focus, Not Broad Generalizations)	
	Link Directly to "Unwrapped" Priority Standards, Not to Curriculum Materials	
	Represent *All* "Unwrapped" Priority Standards Collectively	

Unit Assessments (Pre-, Post-, During Unit)

	Essential Element	Comment(s) / Feedback
	Represent *Blend* of Selected-Response (Multiple Choice) and Constructed-Response (Short and Extended)	
	Include Explicit, Complete Student Directions	
	Clear, Concise Language; Bias-Free for All Students	
	Valid (Measure What Intended to Measure); *Reliable* (Produce Consistent Student Responses Over Time)	
	Directly Align to "Unwrapped" Concepts, Skills, Levels of Bloom's Taxonomy and Depth of Knowledge (DOK)	
	Match Levels of Rigor in "Unwrapped" Skills (e.g., Analyze, Analysis Question; Interpret, Interpretation Question)	
	Match Format and Rigor of Common Core Sample Assessment Items (SBAC/PARCC)	
	Include Proper Academic Vocabulary, Not Simplified Terms (e.g., "Hypothesis," Not "Educated Guess")	
	Provide Evidence Whether Unit's "Unwrapped" Concepts, Skills Have/Have Not Been Learned	
	Assessment Questions Meet Established Criteria for Quality* *See "Evaluating Items" Document (Appendix C)	

Unit Assessments (Pre-, Post-, During Unit) *(continued)*	
Pre-Assessment: *Aligned* (Directly Matched to Post-Assessment but with Fewer Questions) or *Mirrored* (Exact Number and Types of Questions as Post-Assessment)	
Progress-Monitoring Checks: Create Short, Ungraded "Checks for Student Understanding" to Administer Throughout Unit of Study; Directly Aligned to Post-Assessment Questions (Selected-, Short-, Extended-Response); Coincide with Learning Progressions—the "Building Block Chunks" of Instruction	

Post-Assessment Completion		
	Essential Element	**Comment(s) / Feedback**
	Confirm Total Number of Questions Appropriate for Grade Level and Reflect Rigor of Unit Priority Standards	
	Provide Answer Key for Selected-Response Section and Scoring Guides for Constructed-Response Sections (*See Scoring Guide Essential Elements below) with a Description of Each Score Point Either in Student or Teacher Language	
	Prepare Student Version of Assessment	
	Provide Completed Assessment in Hard Copy and Electronic Formats	
	Include List of Needed Assessment Materials and Where Obtained (e.g., Articles, Web Links, Poems, Book Titles, Videos)	
	Provide Administration Directions, Supplemental Information for Teachers to Foster Easy Replication	
	Include Suggested Time Frame for Administering and Scoring Assessment	
	Suggest Potential Accommodations (Changes in How Students Can Acquire Information, Process Information, and/or Demonstrate Learning) Based on Readiness or Individual Student Learning Profile	
	Include Examples of Student Work to Accompany Each Section to Assist Teacher Scoring of Assessments (Optional)	
	Include Assessment Design Team Suggestions and Field Notes for Teachers Who Will Use	

Engaging Scenario

	Essential Element	Comment(s) / Feedback
	Establishes the "Why" for Learning	
	Sets Relevant and Authentic (Real-World) Context for Learning "Unwrapped" Concepts and Skills	
	Motivates Students to Engage in Tasks	
	Includes All SCRAP Criteria (Situation; Challenge; Role; Audience; Product or Performance)	

Authentic Performance Tasks

	Essential Element	Comment(s) / Feedback
	Tasks (3 to 5) Distributed Throughout Unit of Study	
	Represent "Assured Learning Experiences" for *All* Students	
	Include Detailed, Explicit, Step-by-Step Student Directions	
	Cognitive Rigor (Bloom/DOK) Increases First to Last Task	
	Advance Students from Literal to Conceptual Understanding	
	Reflect Rigor of "Unwrapped" Priority Standards (i.e., Analyze, Analysis Task; Evaluate, Evaluation Task, etc.)	
	Authentic and Challenging for All Students	
	Incorporate Unit's Supporting Standards	
	Integrate Interdisciplinary Connections	
	Emphasize 21st-Century Learning Skills	
	Provide Key Teaching Points Pertinent to Each Task	
	Suggest Specific Instructional Strategies for Each Performance Task to Meet Individual Student Needs	
	Student Work Products Provide Evidence of Student Learning	
	Collectively "Deliver" Students to Discovery of Unit Big Ideas	

Scoring Guides

	Essential Element	Comment(s) / Feedback
	Use with Short-Response, Extended-Response, Big Idea Reponses to Essential Questions, and Performance Tasks	
	Represent Multiple Levels of Achievement (e.g., Advanced, Goal, Proficient, Progressing, Beginning)	
	Use Specific, Observable, Measurable Criteria Understood by Students, Teachers, Parents to Ensure Reliability	
	Emphasize Advanced- and Goal/Proficient-Level Criteria; Below-Proficient Levels Refer Back to Goal/Proficient Level	
	Criteria Match Task Requirements (i.e., "Hand-to-Glove Fit"—Student Directions and Scoring Guide Criteria Match)	
	Include Combination of Quantitative *and* Qualitative Criteria; Wording Reflects Rigor of Standards and Tasks	
	Reveal Students' Degree of Proficiency Relative to Targeted Standards	
	Enable Students to Self-Monitor Progress and Receive Timely Feedback for Improving Quality Of Work	

Materials / Resources

	Essential Element	Comment(s) / Feedback
	Include Suggested and/or Required Lists of Needed Instructional Materials and Where Obtained (e.g., Articles, Web sites, Text Selections, Teacher-Created Resources, Technology Hardware and Software)	
	Resources Support Range of Culturally Relevant Student Learning Needs; Resources Equip Students to Succeed	

Differentiation Strategies

	Essential Element	Comment(s) / Feedback
	Suggest Specific Strategies for Research-Based Instructional Strategies; 21st-Century Skills; Intervention Strategies; Specially Designed Instruction (Special Education); and English Language Learners (ELL)	
	Suggest Variety of Accommodations in General (Changes in How Students Can Acquire Information, Process Information, and/or Demonstrate Learning)	
	Suggest How to Accommodate Individual Student Differences (Learning Styles, Skill Levels, Interests) Through Variety of Strategies, Approaches	

Vocabulary

	Essential Element	Comment(s) / Feedback
	Includes Blend of Vocabulary Essential for Life and for Understanding of Content: • *Content-Specific* Words Applicable to Area of Study • *General Academic* Words Occurring in Text or Conversation • Words Used In Daily Conversation	
	Identifies Both *Academic* Vocabulary of Standards and Additional Content Vocabulary *Specific* to Unit	
	Provides Common Definitions for Each Academic Term	

Remediation and Enrichment

	Essential Element	Comment(s) / Feedback
	Considers Needs of Students with Disabilities	
	Considers Needs of English Language Learners	
	Builds Background Knowledge	
	Provides Relearn/Recovery Options	
	Provides Opportunities to Accelerate and Enrich Learning	

Additional Comments

Evaluating Items for Alignment, Frequency, and Quality

Activity 1: Check for Alignment

Use the following Priority Standards **alignment** questions to guide the design group's discussions.

1. *How many of our assessment items align? Which ones?*

2. *How many of our assessment items do **not** align? Which ones?*

3. *Do all of our assessment items directly match the "unwrapped" concepts and skills of the targeted Priority Standards?*

4. *Do our assessment items match the level of the rigor required by the higher-level "unwrapped" Priority Standard skills, such as "evaluate" or "analyze"?*

5. *Do all of our assessment items use the same terms that appear in the standards as opposed to more student-friendly wording (e.g., "identify" rather than "label")?*

6. *Do all of our assessment items align with or resemble the formatting of our district and state assessments so that such formats will be familiar to students?*

7. *What does this tell us? Are our assessment items matched to our intended instructional purposes (the targeted "unwrapped" Priority Standards)?*

8. *What do we need to do next in this regard? Which items do we keep? Which items do we need to replace or modify so that they do align with our Priority Standards?*

Activity 2: Check for Frequency

Use the following Priority Standards **frequency** questions to guide the design group's discussions.

1. *How **many** of our assessment items match each Priority Standard?*

2. *Are certain Priority Standards **under**represented? Which ones?*

3. *Are certain Priority Standards **over**represented? Which ones?*

4. *Are we trying to address too many Priority Standards in this one assessment?*

5. *What does this tell us? Do we need to redistribute our assessment items so that the appropriate number of Priority Standards is more equally represented?*

6. *What do we need to do next in this regard? Which items do we keep as is? Which items do we need to replace or modify so that there is a better balance between the actual number of items and each of our targeted Priority Standards?*

Activity 3: Identify Assessment Types

Use the following **assessment-type** questions to guide the design group's discussions.

1. *Which type(s) of assessment did we include (multiple-choice, short-answer, extended-response)?*

2. *Which other type(s) might we consider using in the revision?*

3. *Which Priority Standards elements ("unwrapped" concepts, skills, and Big Ideas) would be best assessed by selected-response? By constructed-response?*

4. *Will our assessment types provide us with "multiple-measure" evidence of student attainment of the targeted Priority Standards?*

5. *What changes do we need to make in this regard?*

Activity 4: Evaluate Assessment Item Quality

Use the following **assessment-quality** questions to guide the design group's discussions.

1. *Which of our assessment items meet established evaluation criteria for quality?*

2. *Which items do **not** meet such criteria and thus need revision?*

3. *Is there a **range** of low-level to high-level thinking and problem-solving skills represented in our assessment items?*

4. *Which low-level items could be revised so that they become higher-level?*

5. *Are all the items fair, unbiased, valid, and reliable? Are they understandable from the students' point of view?*

6. *Will data from these assessment items **inform** instruction as to what students truly need to know and be able to do with regard to these Priority Standards concepts and skills **in time** for us to make needed changes?*

Activity 5: Develop an Action Plan for Improvements

Discuss with your team members the following questions and then record your responses in an action plan to be shared with your administrators.

1. *When will we revise our assessments, using the revision notes we have made today? Record suggestions: "late start" days; substitute teachers during school day; contract pay for after-school, weekend, or summer work; and so on.*

2. *Who in our department or grade level will do the actual revision work?*

3. *What information, assistance, and/or resources do we need to accomplish this?*

4. *When can we reasonably expect these revisions to be completed?*

5. *When will we administer our **revised** common formative assessments?*

Source: L. Ainsworth and D. Viegut, *Common Formative Assessments: How to Connect Standards-Based Instruction and Assessment,* Chapter 6, pp. 63–75, Corwin Press, 2006.

References

Ainsworth, L. (2003a). *Power standards: Identifying the standards that matter the most.* Englewood, CO: Lead + Learn Press.

Ainsworth, L. (2003b). *"Unwrapping" the standards: A simple process to make standards manageable.* Englewood, CO: Lead + Learn Press.

Ainsworth, L. (2010). *Rigorous curriculum design: How to create curricular units of study that align standards, instruction, and assessment.* Englewood, CO: Lead + Learn Press.

Ainsworth, L., & Viegut, D. J. (2006). *Common formative assessments: How to connect standards-based instruction and assessment.* Thousand Oaks, CA: Corwin Press.

Anderson, L. W., & Krathwohl, D. R., eds. (2001). *A taxonomy for learning, teaching and assessing: A revision of Bloom's taxonomy of educational objectives.* New York: Longman.

Bloom, B. S., et al. (1956). *The taxonomy of educational objectives: Handbook I, cognitive domain.* New York: David McKay.

DuFour, R., & Eaker, R. (1998). *Professional learning communities at work: Best practices for enhancing student achievement.* Bloomington, IN: Solution Tree.

DuFour, R., & Marzano, R. (2011). *Leaders of learning: How district, school, and classroom leaders improve student achievement.* Bloomington, IN: Solution Tree.

Flach, Tracey. (2011). *Engaging students through performance assessment: Creating performance tasks to monitor student learning.* Englewood, CO: Lead + Learn Press.

Hess, K. (2006). *Cognitive complexity: Applying Webb DOK levels to Bloom's taxonomy.* Dover, NH: National Center for Assessment.

Hess, K. (2012). *Exploring cognitive demand in instruction and assessment.* Dover, NH: National Center for Assessment.

Hollingsworth, J., & Ybarra, S. (2009). *Explicit direct instruction (EDI): The power of the well-crafted, well-taught lesson.* Thousand Oaks, CA: Corwin Press.

Leadership and Learning Center, The. (2006). *Common formative assessments.* 1st ed. Englewood, CO: Lead + Learn Press.

Leadership and Learning Center, The. (2008). *Decision making for results.* Englewood, CO: Lead + Learn Press.

Leadership and Learning Center, The. (2009a). *Engaging classroom assessments: The making standards work series.* Englewood CO: Lead + Learn Press.

Leadership and Learning Center, The. (2009b). *Power strategies for effective teaching.* 1st ed. Englewood, CO: Lead + Learn Press.

Leadership and Learning Center, The. (2010a). *Data teams.* 3rd ed. Englewood, CO: Lead + Learn Press.

Leadership and Learning Center, The. (2010b). *Rigorous curriculum design.* 1st ed. Englewood, CO: Lead + Learn Press.

Lemov, D. (2010). *Teach like a champion: 49 techniques that put students on the path to college.* San Francisco, CA: Jossey-Bass.

Marzano, R. J. (2003). *What works in schools: Translating research into action.* Alexandria, VA: Association for Supervision and Curriculum Development.

Marzano, R. J., Norford, J. S., Paynter, D. E., Pickering, D. J., & Gaddy, B. B. (2001). *A handbook for classroom instruction that works.* Alexandria, VA: Association for Supervision and Curriculum Development.

Marzano, R. J., Pickering, D. J., & Pollock, J. E. (2001). *Classroom instruction that works.* Alexandria, VA: Association for Supervision and Curriculum Development.

National Education Association (NEA). (2003). *Balanced assessment: The key to accountability and improved student learning.* Washington, DC: National Education Association.

OECD. (2005). *Formative assessment: Improving learning in secondary classrooms.* Retrieved from http://www.oecd.org/edu/ceri/35661078.pdf

Popham, W. J. (2003). *Test better, teach better: The instructional role of assessment.* Alexandria, VA: Association for Supervision and Curriculum Development.

Reeves, D. B. (2000). *Accountability in action: A blueprint for learning organizations.* Englewood, CO: Lead + Learn Press.

Reeves, D. B. (2002a). *The leader's guide to standards: A blueprint for educational equity and excellence.* San Francisco, CA: Jossey-Bass.

Reeves, D. B. (2002b). *Making standards work: How to implement standards-based assessments in the classroom, school, and district.* 3rd ed. Englewood, CO: Lead + Learn Press.

Schmoker, M. (2011). *Focus: Elevating the essentials to radically improve student learning.* Alexandria, VA: Association for Supervision and Curriculum Development.

Webb, N. (2002). *Depth-of-knowledge levels for four content areas.* Unpublished paper.

Index